Krautrock Eruption

First published in German language 2016 by Ventil Verlag

ISBN 978-3-95575-233-0
Second edition April 2025

© 2025 Ventil Verlag UG (haftungsbeschränkt) & Co. KG,
Boppstr. 25, D-55118 Mainz, produkt@ventil-verlag.de
Use of this material, in full or in part, is only permitted with
expressly agreement of the publisher. All rights reserved.

 In Cooperation with Tapete Records

Design: Oliver Schmitt
Print & binding: maincontor GmbH

www.ventil-verlag.de

Wolfgang Seidel

KRAUTROCK ERUPTION

An Alternative History of German Underground
in the 60s and 70s

With a commented discography
of selected krautrock records
by Holger Adam

Translation
by Alexander Paulick

Wolfgang Seidel with Ton Steine Scherben, 1971

Wolfgang Seidel was born in a West Berlin backyard in 1949. He survived the first half of the 1960s thanks to science fiction novels he bought with his meager pocket money and the music broadcast by the Allied broadcasters AFN and BBC. Music that was a promise that there had to be more and better things out there than post-war Germany. Seidel was one of the founders of Ton Steine Scherben in 1970. Since the mid-1980s he has worked in Berlin as a graphic designer and is active as a drummer and electronics engineer with Alfred Harth, among others, in improvised music.

Holger Adam is one of the co-editors of German magazine *testcard – Beiträge zur Popgeschichte*.

CONTENTS

We have to get out of here ... 8 • Protecting the youth 15 • If you don't behave, you'll be sent to a home ... 17 • Signals of rebellion 19 • A happy family 21 • A roof over their heads 25 • This is our house 26 • Weeds from the ruins 29 • As long as the name starts with The 33 • From beat to krautrock 34 • Cosmic music 40 • Avant-garde and electronic music 41 • Karlheinz Stockhausen 44 • The sound of kraut – the Ruhr region 48 • Frankfurt 52 • Hamburg 54 • Munich 57 • Everywhere & nowhere 58 • West Berlin 60 • Noise and infinite spaces 68 • Synthetic music 69 • The motorik beat 73 • Jazz 79 • Free jazz 99 • Totally free music 102 • Speechless 106 • Beat-Club, re-education and Sexpol 110 • Intermedia and song days 116 • Underground? Pop? Nein! Gegenkultur! 120 • Drawing a clear dividing line ... 124 • The enemy in your own bed 129 • The true, the beautiful, the good ... 132 • Art & artificiality 138 • Rebirth of Germany 142 • Krautrock forever 147 • Future Days 149

Agree to disagree – A selected krautrock discography 163
Photo credits 186

As a child in the 1950s, I was fascinated by my aunt's portable radio, which must have once belonged to one of the US soldiers stationed in West Berlin. It looked different to the radios I knew from other family living rooms, which had a polished wooden casing, golden decorations and gold brocade concealing the loudspeaker. Those radios looked like old-fashioned pieces of furniture and hid their technology like something dangerous that you wouldn't want to have in your own home. In contrast, my aunt's radio was a cross between an American road cruiser and a spaceship from one of the science fiction films that hit the cinemas in the 1950s. A huge display showed the shortwave band with the names of distant places, and a world map with time zones was in the flipped-up lid. The radio was the promise that there was a world out there, a world outside the grey, enclosed West Berlin where I grew up. The radio not only proudly presented itself as an object of advanced technology, it also made it clear that the places I longed for could be reached via this technology. This longing was not limited to the earth. Listening to shortwave at night, in a room lit only by the glow of the valves and the magic eye of the receiver, not only brought voices from distant places, ships and aeroplanes – shortwave reception, with all its interference, also conveyed a sense of the distance between transmitter and receiver. The strange sounds seemed to connect the listener with the stars.

WE HAVE TO GET OUT OF HERE ...

Few phrases summarise the attitude to life of young people in Germany in the 1960s and 1970s better than this one: "We have to get out of here!" Out of a Germany that demanded one thing above all else from young people: to keep their mouths shut and adapt smoothly to the discipline of school and work (and, for young men, military service, which was reintroduced in West Germany in 1955). And this within a country in which the last traces of the consequences of that sort of discipline had only just been cleared away, and the leading personnel in business, politics, administration, the judiciary, and the military were largely identical to those before 1945. Even the minor authorities, the teachers, instructors, and heads of families, were largely moulded by the same ideology, which demanded submission and conformity from young people. This applied to both West and East Germany. As a young person, you only had one wish: to get out.

For young people in the West, there were several ways to escape the disciplinary grip on body and mind. You could drop out completely and wander around Europe as a drifter with a sleeping bag and a few books, heading north in the summer, where the air and love were freer, and chasing the sun in the winter, heading south. You could study philosophy for 40 semesters and avoid any economic exploitation. You could move to a rural commune, although you could only rarely live off the land. In most cases, you had to make a living from what you earned in the city or what your parents sent you. Or you could escape to drug paradises. Either with the help of the latest products from the Sandoz chemical laboratories into the vastness of the cosmos – not only because of the general enthusiasm for space travel. The future was still terra incognita, free of all identitarian attributions and prefabricated lifestyles. Another way out was to leave German normality behind with the medicine chest of a romanticised Orient. However, this harboured the risk of not only unintentionally connecting with obscure gurus, but also with a romantic anti-modernism, which was not entirely free of the misery from which one wanted to escape. Those who were serious about it made their way to the promised land of India and Afghanistan. As a rule, however, the hard labour in the poppy fields was left to the locals.

The years 1967/68 were something of a watershed in terms of drug use, as with many other things. Previously, stimulants had been the drug of choice for young members of the working class and lower middle class, for whom social advancement in the golden age of Rhineland capitalism seemed to be guaranteed. You could dance the entire weekend away on this stuff, and celebrate your own small part in the economic miracle. With the rapid politicisation of youth, the question of the drug of choice also became a political issue. Alcohol and amphetamines were regarded either as narcotics or performance-enhancing drugs, and were accordingly viewed critically. On the other hand, so-called mind-expanding drugs were seen as a way of overcoming capitalist normality, with its cycle of production, wage labour and consumption. At the beginning of the 1970s, when it became clear that the resistance was greater and the leaden years of the hunt for terrorists cast their shadows ahead, the use of narcotic drugs increased. The back-to-back deaths of Janis Joplin, Jimi Hendrix and Jim Morrison could have been more than a coincidence, or they were perhaps a symptom of this shift in climate. There was also a fair amount of recklessness involved. "Once you tell a lie, you're never believed." The authorities had told so many frightful stories about all the horrors that would follow that first joint, but which never materialised, so even justified warnings were thrown to the wind.

Another sign of the fatigue that followed the optimistic decade of the 1960s, was the shift from the anti-authoritarian movement to the formation of left-wing parties that followed the old model of the Leninist cadre party. While heroin was a problem for young people who otherwise hardly had much to expect from life due to their social background, membership of one of these "workers'" parties was more for middle class children. They wished to escape their privileged background and become members of one of the communist parties working for the benefit of the proletariat and world revolution. These groups disbanded at some point because the revolution failed to materialise, and there were hardly any proletarians who had enough trust in their bosses' children to join in the first place.

But before that happened, everything seemed possible. Published in 2014, *We Thought We Could Change the World* is the title of a volume of interviews with Peter Brötzmann, one of the most radical musical rebels of the 1960s. The sentence reflects the mood of a time that would later be labelled "'68". It had already begun a few years earlier. There is no cut-off date for this development, neither for its beginning nor for the fading of the spirit of optimism, which turned 180 degrees in the second half of the 1970s with the slogan "No Future".

The desire to get out gripped a youth that could have actually found it easy to get in. Precarious employment and the Hartz IV benefits scheme were still decades in the future. You didn't have to worry if your A-level average was worse than a 1.5. Turbo A-levels and bachelor's degrees were unheard of, and even skilled workers could look forward to their future in a terraced house with an adjoining party cellar with some peace of mind. While social mobility was as low as it is today until the 1950s, unusual opportunities for advancement opened up for a few years. This was due to gaps left by the war, which made labour a scarce resource that companies had to compete for. Added to this was the technological push, which demanded highly qualified personnel. The demands of critical young people for training reforms thus coincided with certain needs of the economy. If you were young back then, you didn't have to worry about your future. If you were young and left-wing, you were sure that the future would eventually bring a worldwide revolution. And until then, you could always go out and get a job.

Left-wing debates, which had previously centred on the exploitation of wage earners, increasingly focused on the question of the alienated life. Not that traditional exploitation had disappeared, but it had been outsourced to guest workers and the Third World. For the skilled German worker, the future looked rosy, with a building society savings contract and a regular income, two weeks holiday in Italy, a terraced house, a wife and two children. The only existential question was the decision: Opel or Ford? It was precisely this secure life, happiness through consumption, that young people were fleeing from. They mistrusted the family idyll, which demanded unquestioning conformity as the price for material security. One reason for this mistrust were the Auschwitz trials in Frankfurt, which brought to light the horror of the extermination camps. The fact that it had taken almost 20 years for the first legal reappraisal to take place also turned this development into a generational conflict, which lent additional energy to the debate. Added to this were the anti-colonial struggles, which raised the question of the extent to which the prosperity of the First World was based on poverty and oppression in the Third World. This culminated in the protests against the war in Vietnam and the military dictatorships in Latin America, where the leading power of the West, which had been seen as a democratic role model, took brutal action against these ideals. At the same time, the USA remained the place of longing that it had been since the wave of emigration in the 19th century. It was also the source of the cultural and political ideas that articulated young people's mistrust of the world they found themselves living in.

Leaving the false family idyll meant, quite practically, moving into a shared flat or commune. People hoped that life in a collective would bring them relief from the psychological wounds and moulding caused by the nuclear family. When the bourgeois citizen heard the word commune, they thought of the worst thing they could imagine after the abolition of private property: free love. Even if love was not as free as the young men and women had hoped, gaining control over their own bodies was a driving force behind this movement. The squares – with their bodies petrified by discipline, who could only escape their armour with a dirty joke at the bar or through an act of violence – were a repellent example to young people. Wolfgang Staudte portrayed them so harshly in his 1951 film adaptation of Heinrich Mann's novel *Der Untertan*, that the film was banned in West Germany for years and was only released after being shortened. The fact that the completely un-emancipatory and temporary breakdown of discipline among the citizens, was usually only possible through alcohol meant that young people avoided the locals at the bar and their latent aggression, preferring to reach for a joint rather than a bottle. This oppressive atmosphere can still be felt in Rainer Werner Fassbinder's early films, such as *Katzelmacher*, or in Peter Fleischmann's *Jagdszenen aus Niederbayern*.

Breaking out of traditional gender roles was another door to the outside world. Even before 1968, a new self-confidence had developed for women as a result of their improved economic situation and the introduction of the contraceptive pill. Young women deliberately celebrated this as a provocation and self-empowerment. The fight over skirt length (short) and men's hair length (long) could become rather violent. At the minimum, angry citizens were already uninhibitedly slobbering their violent fantasies into television microphones. What began as individual protest, led to the emerging women's movement. It combined feminism with a radical critique of capitalism, and demanded far more than just legal or economic equality.

The easiest way out was with a record player or a radio. The record player was better, because the dominance of German popular music on the radio was unbroken until the end of the 1960s. If you ask people whose youth landed in the decade between 1962 and 1972 about their favourite music, The Beatles and The Rolling Stones usually come out on top. Songs that became memorable had titles that were programmatic: "Break On Through (To the Other Side)" by The Doors, "My Generation" by The Who, or "(I Can't Get No) Satisfaction" by The Rolling Stones. But even songs whose lyrics offered no impetus for a rebellious statement, such as The Kinks' "You Really Got Me", were still a clear incitement to rise up, thanks to the raw power of their guitar riffs. This was enhanced by the androgynous dandyism of The Kinks, who represented the exact opposite of the proper, soldierly man.

Film was another door to the outside world (probably the most important one before the beat music wave), but you couldn't do more than imitate the dress code and poses of the stars. The beauty of music, on the other hand, was that you could enjoy it actively. With the arrival of the first Beatles and Stones records, bands were formed everywhere and emulated this sound. In the beginning, for most of them it was purely a leisure activity, but it was only towards the end of the 1960s that the fun was combined with the discourses of the new left, and being in a band became a vehicle for the dream of non-alienated labour. This marriage of music and politics was not a matter of course. Nor was it something that most of the musicians had consciously intended. The political message was something that the fans projected onto it. The reaction of the state, schools and parents also contributed to the politicisation of pop music. Having fun, especially having fun being different, was an offence in a country shaped by a conformist ideology.

The first clashes between young people and the police had no specific political cause. They were Bill Haley's performances at the end of the 1950s, The Rolling Stones' concert at the Waldbühne in West Berlin in 1966 and the Schwabing riots in Munich in 1962, which were triggered by the expulsion of a group of street musicians by the police. Several thousand young people took part in the ensuing street battles with the police. There were also clashes between beat fans and state power in the GDR, where the repressive authorities cracked down with all their might. After that, music that ran counter to the prevailing ideology could only exist in the underground – where the word underground was more than just an advertising label. The old left had great difficulty understanding the new youth movement. The authoritarian communist parties in the East were suspicious from the outset of any grassroots movement that was not under their control.

And the fact that these parties had severed their ties with the artistic avant-garde in the 1930s took its toll on them. Instead, a concept of culture was proclaimed that was nationalistically charged, culminating in Ulbricht's statement that there was no need for any "foreign Yeah Yeah". The GDR's state radio committee called for the promotion of "national intonation". This had nothing to do with Adorno's critique of the culture industry. It drew on the national resentment and anti-Americanism of the old educated classes, and acted as the custodian of "good Prussian virtues" while the West was denounced as an American colony. The propaganda success with the bourgeoisie, hoped for as allies, was limited, and the GDR lost the youth for good.

PROTECTING THE YOUTH

Anyone who does a bit of television archaeology and watches a pseudo-documentary crime series with plenty of local colour, such as *Stahlnetz* from the early 1960s, will notice one thing missing in them: young people. There are children and unready, mostly awkward young adults. Youth as an increasingly longer, independent phase of life with its own cultural expression had not yet been invented. When young people did appear, it was as halfwitted delinquents, seduced by bad, mostly American role models – almost as a criminal offence in their own right. They were characterised by an unsoldierly posture, a desire to consume and, above all, flippant answers with which they challenged the authorities. Another recurring feature was the use of Anglicisms in music, clothing and language, almost as if they were the second wave of GIs bringing the occupying regime into schools and families.

The desire for dissidence was a reaction to a discipline and a graveyard calm that, when encountered today in German films or television productions from the 1950s, seems almost comical. For those affected, it was not. As a young person, you were subject to constant monitoring and were only really unsuspicious if you remained invisible. The "Law for the Protection of Youth" contained numerous restrictions on freedom of movement. It reflected the mindset of orderly Germans, who saw young people as a threat or felt they needed to be protected from such – which amounted to the same thing. The law came into force in 1952 and was partly characterised by the spirit of Heinrich Himmler's "Police Ordinance for the Protection of Youth", which had been in force until then. The Nazi decree of 1943 stated: "Due to the changed living conditions caused by the war, the following is decreed for the protection of youth (…): §1) Keep away from public streets and squares or other public places during the hours of darkness – Minors under the age of 18 are not allowed to loiter on public streets and squares or in other public places during the hours of darkness." And in paragraph 5, the fun for young people came to a complete end: "Minors aged 16 to 18 are only permitted to stay in rooms where public dance parties are held and to participate in public dance parties indoors and outdoors if accompanied by a parent or guardian or their authorised representative until 11 pm."

The name of the ordinance was cynical, as the young people to be protected were conscripted into the Wehrmacht when they reached the age of 18. This not only put an abrupt end to youth; for many, life ended just as suddenly a few weeks later in a trench somewhere in the Soviet Union. Accordingly, there was a great need to savour what little youth they possessed and to ignore the rules. Then came the post-war years, in which life only slowly returned to normal. First, the rubble had to be cleared away and the bare necessities for survival organised. Children and young people were largely left to their own devices, with huge fields of rubble as their playground. This freedom and the independence they discovered was soon to be taken away from them again.

IF YOU DON'T BEHAVE, YOU'LL BE SENT TO A HOME ...

The harshest measure for disciplining young people was being sent to a home, or a boarding school for the children of the upper classes. But there is nothing cosy about this kind of home. They were prisons for children and young people, where they were sent at the request of their parents – "If you don't behave, you'll be sent to a home!" – or at the instigation of the youth welfare offices. There, children and young people were disciplined with physical violence, locked up and used for involuntary unpaid labour. In addition to exploitation as cheap labour, there were also numerous cases of sadistic violence and sexual abuse. There was no monitoring of the admissions practice or of these homes, 70 percent of which were run by the major churches. The fact that this system, to which around 800,000 children fell victim, was able to function until the 1970s, was due to the definition of antisocial behaviour and difficulty of education adopted from National Socialism. It was not only the ideology that was adopted. The authoritative personnel responsible for institutionalisation, and in the homes themselves, were often the same as they were before 1945. They simply carried on, sometimes in the same buildings that had served as prisons or camps during National Socialism, with inmates who had to wear the same prisoner clothes. Ulrike Meinhof undertook her research into youth homes in 1971, as seen in the television film *Bambule*, which promptly disappeared into the archives for 20 years. Her look beneath the surface of the Federal Republic of Germany, which celebrated itself as an economic miracle nation, may have contributed to Meinhof's radicalisation and her path to the Red Army Faction. It was not until 2012 that the German government managed to recognise, not even half-heartedly, the injustice caused by the repressive system of these homes. The reform of residential care in the 1970s was the result of the "home campaign" of the anti-authoritarian movement, which not only denounced home care from the late 1960s onwards, but also supported young people who escaped from institutions.

"As long as your legs remain under my table ..." was one of the slogans used to discipline youngsters. It was particularly effective for pupils and students who had no income of their own. Those who were doing a vocational training programme didn't have it much better, because "apprenticeship years are not master years". Most apprentices were employed in small businesses, where they were above all one thing: cheap labour. The standard of training was poor unless you were lucky enough to have found an apprenticeship in a large company with its own training workshop. There was only a minimal apprenticeship payment, which often had to be handed over to the parents except for a meagre amount of pocket money. In Clemens Kuby's 1972 film *Lehrlinge* (with music by Ton Steine Scherben), the protagonist of the story sums up the situation: "At work I'm not allowed to say anything, and at home I have to keep my mouth shut."

SIGNALS OF REBELLION

In Germany, the economic recovery from the consequences of the war was so rapid that the term "economic miracle" was soon being bandied about. However, the ideological structures and their practical and legal effects on everyday life remained in place. The ideological struggle even seemed to intensify the more this ideology came into conflict with economic development. The common term for the political and counter-cultural movements of the 1960s is student revolt – but this is misleading. Even the magical date of '68 is only partially accurate. In the same way, the shooting of student Benno Ohnesorg by a West Berlin police officer on the 2nd of June 1967, could be seen as the decisive date upon which a long-in-the-making development reached a critical mass. The fact that students played an important role in the protest and modernisation movements also had to do with the change in the number and composition of the student body, into which more children of upwardly mobile workers and employees were moving. The number of students enrolled at universities had tripled. The opposition to authoritarian structures had already started in the years before 1968 and was supported by young workers for whom the central issue was not the war in Vietnam, but their own living conditions at school and work. In 1968 there were fierce clashes with the state in Bremen over a planned fare increase for local public transport, in which the works councils of the shipyards and steelworks also showed solidarity with the demonstrators.

If it had purely been a student protest at the time, it would all be long forgotten today. Striking students do not have the same social and, above all, economic impact as striking workers. Although the dreamed-of revolution failed to materialise, some things did change: there was criminal law reform, shorter working hours, legal equality of the sexes, and the abolition of Paragraph 175, which criminalised homosexuality. Above all, everyday life and the way people treated each other changed. If you compare street scenes, clothing, and body language in old films from the 1950s and early 1960s with scenes shot after 1970, you get a sense of how profound these changes were; even if they often happened with a lot of resistance, compromise and, primarily, agonisingly slow legal implementation. The fact that this was possible at all was due to a coalition of schoolchildren, apprentices, and students that had not previously existed and who communicated mainly through the medium of music. Even if reality lagged behind, the ideal was a youth without class distinctions, listening to the same bands and wearing the same jeans. In *Beat in Liverpool*, one of the first books on this new youth culture, the authors Juergen Seuss, Gerold Dommermuth and Hans Maier write that the youth "in their protest behaviour, is a society divided into often hostile groupings, yet is almost classless in its approach. Although it can be roughly said that the intellectual beatniks and layabouts often come from the upper and middle classes, the mods and beat fans often from the lower middle class, and the rockers from the working class, the exceptions and points of contact between these groups are so numerous, and the behaviour towards established values so similar, that any such classification becomes rather questionable."

In the fight against authoritarian structures and repressive sexual morals, pupils, apprentices, and students found themselves in the same position. Together, they developed forms of action that gave this movement the necessary impetus. In addition, the early 1970s saw the largest strike movement in the history of the Federal Republic of Germany, which was not only about higher wages, but also about improved working conditions, co-determination and shorter working hours. Increases in productivity were so notable that this seemed possible and necessary. The trade union leaders in Germany, who were notoriously unwilling to fight, had to adapt to this zeitgeist as they ran the risk of losing control over their members and, most importantly, over the radicalising youth trade unionists. Added to this was the influence of the so-called guest worker colleagues from southern Europe, who brought with them a different, more radical tradition of industrial action.

A HAPPY FAMILY

The struggle between reactionaries and reformers not only took place in school classes, seminars, apprentice workshops, or in public spaces. Another arena of this struggle was the patriarchally structured family. It had been affected by the war, as the men had been away for a long time and had not returned victorious. We can speak of a traumatised generation – young men of an age to fall in love, who instead had gone out to kill. This generation initially fell into silence. If a narrative existed at all, it was the precursor to the role of victim that has become widespread in recent years. Nobody talked about what they had hoped for from the ideal final victory – an estate in the Ukraine with slave labourers and maidservants who could be disposed of at will? Utopian visions of what was to come after the glorious final victory are few and far between. Those who study Nazi cultural production, on the other hand, find an aesthetic of (heroic) death.

In the United States and Great Britain, the economic constraints of the war economy had caused traditional gender roles to change. The poster image of "Rosie the Riveter", the cheerfully self-confident worker in blue overalls, is still present in popular cultural memory and constantly reappears in new contexts. In the USA, a lot of effort was put into advertising the fact that women were hired by defence companies. And the advertising had to be good, because there was no obligation to work. Women had to be offered something – and not just money. In advertising films, you see cheerful, well-dressed women working with the latest technology. The promise of adventure, self-determination and social advancement, with which work was made palatable to young women, set in motion a development that was difficult to reverse after the war. The situation was similar in Great Britain. The Royal Air Force was so short of personnel that it employed female pilots. In a BBC documentary 50 years later, these women say that, despite all the dangers, this was the best time of their lives. Above all, they loved the freedom they enjoyed on the ground – including sexual freedom.

These were experiences that also had a lasting effect on emerging pop culture. However, in West Germany in the 1950s and 1960s, these changes were slow to materialise: a character like Emma Peel from the British TV series *The Avengers* could not have been created in Germany. There was only Frau Keller – the wife of Inspector Keller from the ZDF TV-series *Der Kommissar* – to bring her husband his felt slippers. In fact, today we are surprised at how many careworn and frustrated female characters populate the then-successful series. Another recurring theme is the conflict between young and old. Several episodes show older, well-off gentlemen who are thrown off course by an encounter with a "hippie girl". Inspector Keller, played by Erik Ode, always appears as the tolerant understander of youth. This seemed downright progressive in a country whose popular culture had created a parallel universe in pop songs, and the most successful German film genre of those years, the Heimatfilm, which denied reality and, especially, the past. The Heimatfilm in particular attempted to conjure up a status quo ante against a backdrop of unspoilt nature, as if the collective rampage of National Socialism had never happened. Instead, we see postcard landscapes in which the forest maiden waits for her prince. Or for the senior physician from the equally best-selling doctor novels. The Heimatfilm manifested the desire not only to make us forget the war, but also to ignore all the drastic socio-economic changes of the post-war period.

The fact that the situation in Germany was different from that in the United States and Great Britain, had reasons that went back to the time before 1945. Although there had also been a huge demand for labour for the war economy, the employment of women was at odds with ideology. National Socialism had set out to undo all the emancipatory successes that the Weimar Republic had brought for women. The model was the woman as a mother, loyal companion and guardian of the household for the warlike man. The youth organisations – the Hitler Youth for boys, and the League of German Girls for girls and young women – prepared young people for their future roles, strictly separated by gender. Wherever possible, National Socialism covered the war economy's labour needs with forced labourers, as this allowed it to combine two goals: exploitation and extermination. However, this was not possible in all areas, which meant that women also advanced into companies and administrations in Germany. In the immediate post-war years, when many men were still prisoners of war, women had to take responsibility for children and daily life by themselves. With the founding of the Federal Republic of Germany, a rollback began on a broad front in order to restore the old gender order – women were reduced to their role as housewives and mothers. In contrast to National Socialism, this housewife was now also a consumer, pouring Rotbäckchen fruit juice for her children and washing her laundry with Weißer Riese detergent, while bringing the floor to a shine with a Kobold vacuum cleaner. At the same time, she thought about how she could entertain her professionally ambitious husband's guests appropriately – with pretzel sticks and Lufthansa Cocktail aperitifs.

Legally, things were no better. Until the mid-1950s, women were only allowed to have their own bank account with their husband's permission, and only from 1976 (!) they were allowed to take up a profession without permission from their husband. The debates about the abortion law, Paragraph 218, which had taken place during the Weimar period, were ruthlessly ended by the Nazis in 1933. For National Socialism, women were merely ennobled mothering machines who had to provide for the reproduction of warriors (or potential future mothers of warriors and war widows-to-be). And as rigorously as the Nazis were against abortion, they were just as merciless in their euthanasia programme against all offspring who did not conform to their racial delusions and, especially, the postulate of utility for the German people. Sexuality outside of its strictly regulated reproductive function was just as taboo before 1945 as it was afterwards. After the masters of creation (men) had run riot in the occupied countries, decency was suddenly the order of the day, to which women had to subordinate themselves. The police kept files on women who did not want to submit once again, with the reference "HWG" denoting "frequently changing sexual intercourse". With the advent of motorisation, it became a popular pastime for

German police officers to search car parks and remote roads at night for lovers who had made themselves comfortable in the back seat. Where else were they supposed to go? Until the criminal law reform at the beginning of the 1970s during Willy Brandt's chancellorship, the "Kuppelei-Paragraf" was still in force, which punished anyone – including parents – who harboured unmarried people "in the facilitation of fornication". This paragraph mainly affected young people who did not have their own home.

A ROOF OVER THEIR HEADS

Housing was scarce after the destruction of the war, and the allocation and rents were sometimes regulated by the state for years to come. Flats were almost only allocated to married people. It was difficult for single people to find a flat, and younger people in particular were met with mistrust. Women were expected to live in their parents' household until marriage. In West Berlin, the situation was somewhat different, as living space was more available to the departure of all those who were either worried about the uncertain political situation in the city, or saw no economic future in the rapidly deindustrialising city. The West Berlin Senate countered the depopulation of the city with all kinds of benefits, especially for young couples, to make moving to Berlin more attractive. These included help in finding accommodation, favourable loans and tax benefits. Wages in West Berlin were subsidised by a so-called Berlin allowance to even out the gap with wages in West Germany. In addition, there were redevelopment areas approved for demolition, especially in the Kreuzberg district. At this stage, it was possible to pay cheap rent in houses that had become increasingly run-down in order to make way for the planned modernisation – if you were prepared to do so without any comfort. When the wrecking ball came, this area became the centre of the squatter movement.

THIS IS OUR HOUSE

Where do you go when you're young and your head is full of ideas and dreams, but your pockets are empty? Even if you had enough pocket money, there wasn't much you could do with it in small towns. In summer, you could meet up in the park or in front of the ice cream parlour, eyed suspiciously by citizens who preferred young people to remain invisible. The living conditions of young people from working-class households, or from what is now called the lower middle class, were not so lavish that they could have escaped into a private sphere. And that only would have worked if the relationship with their parents' generation had been less fraught. That's why, in 1971, a group of young people occupied an empty factory in West Berlin and turned it into a self-managed communication centre – until they were evicted by the police. The next spectacular action was the occupation of part of the disused Bethanien hospital, which offered young people self-managed accommodation under the name Georg-von-Rauch-Haus. At the events where supporters gathered, the band Ton Steine Scherben played, singing the "Rauch-Haus-Song" and its slogan "Das ist unser Haus" (This is our House), which became something like a squatters' anthem. At the beginning of the 1970s, there quickly emerged a movement of squatters and the founding of autonomous youth centres, which was not limited to the big cities, but also spread to smaller towns where the situation for young people and the leisure options were even more bleak.

Occupying an empty factory or being given rooms by the city – often with the compromise of accepting professional social workers as a supervisory body – was only the first step. The attempt at long-term self-organisation often revealed that the interests of the young people involved were divergent. The seemingly classless society propagated by youth culture was in reality characterised by class differences. These were evident in the fact that ideas of self-determined leisure time or, as in the case of the Rauch House in West Berlin, living together were not obviously compatible among apprentices, young workers, those on the go, secondary school pupils, and students. Apprentices and young workers in particular, for whom the youth centre was a free space to hang out and listen to music away from family control, quickly felt dominated by the more articulate high school and university students, and their endless discussions. The Rauch House, which still exists today, solved the problem by throwing out the students and urging those young people who had run away – either from the family home or from youth care facilities – to either go to school or start an apprenticeship, depending on their age.

At the end of the 1960s, the idea of shared flats or, even more radically, communes, spread rapidly. Shared housing seemed to be the ideal strategy for overcoming isolation and authoritarian education with all its manipulation. Many such flat-sharing communities emerged, and not only in the student milieu. Whether involuntarily or not, the media helped to spread these ideas. Lurid newspaper reports, which were intended to shock or enrage the establishment, had the opposite effect on young people. Television did the same and became a multiplier for the general politicisation of young people. Süddeutscher Rundfunk (SDR) launched *Jour Fix* on television, a magazine programme for "pupils, apprentices and young workers", which reported in detail on these first squats – with astounding success. The editorial team received mountains of letters from young people asking for more information and contact addresses. The programme developed into a communication platform for young people, particularly from small towns, who had similar problems and were now organising themselves to fight for self-managed youth centres – even to the point of squatting, if the authorities responsible for municipal planning did not help to pacify the situation beforehand and make rooms available. What was special about the programme was that it did not report on young people – the young people themselves had the floor and reported in long, barely edited shots about the overarching discipline, both at school or apprenticeships as well as during their free time, where they were not allowed to be free. Yet it wasn't just talk: young people organised themselves.

The programme ran into difficulties precisely because of its success and high viewing figures among the target group. After seven episodes, it was over. In a final, eighth episode, professional social workers and political representatives (Heiner Geißler was responsible as Minister of Social Affairs in Rhineland-Palatinate at the time) were to debate young people in a panel discussion in the tried and tested format. Around 200 of them were invited – as spectators. In addition, one of the bands that is largely forgotten today was scheduled to entertain the audience: Franz K. But the young people refused to be fobbed off with their intended role as a backdrop for a few camera pans. The politicians' routine appeasements and empty phrases did not go down well either. The audience took the initiative, sent representatives to the podium and was not quiet in other ways. The event was reorganised. What sounds like a failure on the part of the programme makers, who were unable to push through their planned concept, was in fact a complete success. After all, the self-empowerment of young people was exactly what *Jour Fix* had reported on and thus had a reinforcing effect. In the first half of the 1970s, there were over 150 of these self-managed youth centres. Although they gradually professionalised if they did not disappear, they were the direct precursor of the squatter movement at the beginning of the 1980s. And just as the squats of the 1980s had their soundtrack in punk, the youth centres of the 1970s were also an important infrastructure for music. Many local bands played there that have long since been forgotten, except for those who at some point emancipated themselves from merely playing English or American material, and began to develop individual styles that from the mid-1970s were gathered under the term krautrock.

WEEDS FROM THE RUINS

The particular potential for conflict that arose from authoritarian structures, the survival of nationalist ideology and the unbroken careers of old Nazis ensured that the question of musical taste, fashion, and lifestyle became much more politically charged in Germany than in other countries. Music played a central role in this, as it made its way into every last village. Beat – as this music was called before terms such as rock and pop became established – musically reflected the optimistic aspiration for a better life in a country where the ghosts of the past still lingered. With music as the central medium, a youthful subculture emerged that linked up early on with political movements such as the protests against nuclear armament. A vast number of bands were formed, enthusiastically emulating their British and American role models.

in *Antipop* Martin Büsser wrote about the atmosphere in which young people lived at the time: "Krautrock was created in a post-fascist, only superficially de-Nazified country in which every deviation from the norm was still punished. Anyone who went out on the street as a man with long hair or a woman with short hair was still at risk of being beaten up." The footage sometimes seen in television documentaries of outraged citizens who lapse into "with Adolf it would have been …" tirades at the sight of long-haired people can only be regarded as a curiosity today. The real threat they posed is no longer comprehensible, although we know that 20 years earlier they had proven that they meant business. Of all things, it was the length of hair that caused people – suitably described by Klaus Theweleit as the "military man" – to fly into a rage because someone was empowering themselves to control their own body instead of subjecting it to the discipline of the factory and the state – a discipline that could wield power over life and death.

The harshness of the conflict perhaps explains why music by German bands labelled as krautrock often has a sense of gloom to it. It also explains why many of the krautrock bands cultivated a particular escapism with which they took refuge in idealised far eastern cultures or fantasised distant pasts. In its actual heyday in the first half of the 1970s, however, krautrock was never widespread enough to be considered a movement. Measured alongside the quantity of music that emerged from the UK and the USA, krautrock was more of a footnote. Krautrock didn't even want to be an independent movement. The musicians saw themselves as part of the transnational counterculture that was labelled "'68". Krautrock is best understood as part of a social movement that revolved around concepts such as non-alienated labour, the critique of capitalism, collective economic forms, self-determination and the incipient debate on ecology. Any attempt to find a consistent musical definition fails due to the heterogeneity of what these bands produced between the late 1960s and mid 1970s. If there is a viable path to a definition, then it is through their embedding in the social environment and the political discourses of those years.

Lothar Meid, bassist with Amon Düül, wrote in the song "Die Helden aus dem Untergrund" (Heros from the Underground): "We came home from school and we listened day and night to the Rolling Stones, the Beatles and old blues, Led Zeppelin and Spooky Tooth. " Which made it clear which bands they aligned themselves with. Amon Düül II's first LP, *Phallus Dei*, was released in 1969 by the German branch of the US label Liberty Records. In its promo text, the record company tried to connect with the zeitgeist, which expected more from a band than just entertaining music: "Amon Düül II sees itself as a symbiotic community." The statement could also be applicable in a press release for an LP by the Grateful Dead or Jefferson Airplane, but in the search for a unique selling point, it then takes on a different tone: "Amon Düül II sees itself as a German group and cultivates the German element in its musical statement. This makes the group's music original and autonomous." Whether this was the idea of the publicity department or the band itself is not clear. In any case, instead of cultivating the supposedly "German element", Amon Düül moved closer and closer to the rock mainstream and, with the exception of the first record, wrote lyrics in English. They were convinced that German, with its harshness, did not suit the music and did not articulate the appropriate distance from German normality. Like many bands in the krautrock scene, Amon Düül took a stand against this by performing at political events. The combination of teach-in and music was widespread at the end of the 1960s and almost all krautrock bands appeared in this context. If there was a "German element", it was in the negation. In their self-portrayal entitled "Was wir waren (unser Weg)", the musicians of Amon Düül write, as Ingrid Schober quotes them in *Tanz der Lemminge*: "In order to overcome the oppression we experienced at the time, we saw music as a free space that enabled us to develop and pursue new forms of communication. We were able to articulate fundamental criticism of the existing system because we had created a model of a counter-society through music."

My early introduction to the church of rock and roll was provided by my sister, who was ten years older than me and had bought a portable radio with her first teaching grant to listen to Frolic at Five on AFN – the American Forces Network. "Heartbreak Hotel" – broken relationships were not yet an issue for me at that age. It was the sound that fascinated me. And there was something else: Until then, the most I had seen of Elvis Presley was in a photo; I hadn't heard the debates about his hip movements, which were described as immoral or animalistic. Nevertheless, there was something about this music that forced you to move with exactly the same soft swing in the hips. It was different from sitting upright on hard wooden benches at school or running round in circles in the school playground at break time like prison inmates.

After work, much to the annoyance of our parents, my sister would hang out with the nightmares of the bourgeoisie – yobs in "Nietenhosen" (that's what blue jeans were called back then) and T-shirts instead of German fine rib underwear. Our parents thought they could restrain my sister by making her look after her little brother. But he made a pact with her: I'll keep my mouth shut and in return I'll go with you everywhere I never would have been allowed to at that tender age. For example, to the fairground, where the bumper car soundtrack consisted of Bill Haley, Ricky Nelson and Elvis Presley.

After rock and roll came the British Invasion. My sister had married in the meantime, but left me her tape recorder. Her tapes of Buddy Holly and the Everly Brothers were now joined by British acts. My cousin, who was a few years older, took me to my first concert. Trini Lopez was announced as the star of the evening, but by then he was already on the wane. The support act left a much more lasting impression. It was the now practically forgotten band The Searchers, who like The Beatles from Liverpool, had a whole string of hits back then. They took to the stage of the Deutschlandhalle, which had a capacity of several thousand people, with three 30-watt suitcase amplifiers – and the hall went wild. Two years later, I was to experience a similar feeling when The Rolling Stones played at the Waldbühne. That time the venue wasn't just boiling, it was boiling over. And above all: It was fun. It was a sensual pleasure.

AS LONG AS THE NAME STARTS WITH THE

Before bands like Amon Düül made a name for themselves, from around 1962 onwards, young people had formed an innumerable mass of bands that rehearsed eagerly in basements. The newly formed local bands practised such perfect mimicry that they disappeared behind the English or

American originals. They were at their best when they were indistinguishable from them. The musicians were mostly amateurs, often still teenagers themselves, and the music was a pastime that combined the excitement of puberty with the excitement of music. They did everything they could to avoid being perceived as German. They had English band names that inevitably started with "The". They sang in English and their sound was oriented towards current British or American trends. If anyone remembers any of them at all today, it's because they were bands that played in the small towns where the tours of the well-known bands didn't go. These were the groups that could be heard at school parties, in the local dance hall or in youth centres for a low entrance price and were paid a correspondingly small fee. Most of them remained at that level and disbanded towards the end of the 1960s. Of those who continued, some emerged from the mimicry of "we'd rather be English" and eventually became what would later be labelled as "krautrock".

FROM BEAT TO KRAUTROCK

"Beatmusik" was a German neologism, and refers to the variant of rock music that originated in England and was adopted by the German bands that had formed. In Germany, on the other hand, the term krautrock was like in Rainer Werner Fassbinder's two-part science fiction film *Welt am Draht* (World on a Wire). Klaus Löwitsch, who plays the cyberneticist Fred Stiller, asks about his missing friend Günther Lause. The answer is always the same: "Who? Günther Lause? Never heard of him!" The film was released in 1973, a time that is said to have been the heyday of krautrock – if you believe British authors such as Julian Cope or David Stubbs. In his 2014 krautrock history *Future Days – Krautrock and the Building of Modern Germany*, Stubbs claims with fan-like enthusiasm that ambient, techno or hip-hop would have been unthinkable without the pioneering work of the krautrockers in the early 1970s. To his amazement, when he visits Germany, Stubbs is like Fred Stiller: "Krautrock? Never heard of it ..." Or krautrock in general – what's that supposed to be? Wikipedia says: "Rock music primarily by West German bands (...) from the late 1960s onwards". However, in 1968, the approximate year of krautrock's birth, the word would have been met with nothing but disapproval – even among the musicians placed in this category. Their categorisation of themselves was either progressive rock, which expressed a wish to keep up with international pop music trends – or free beat. The latter label, which could be found on posters and in articles in music magazines and numerous underground papers, has been forgotten today. But it is much more accurate. Not only does it refer to the free jazz that had emerged a few years earlier; free beat contains the programmatic claim to break away from traditional structures – and not only in the music. Free jazz shared the importance of improvisation, ignoring existing musical conventions and cultivating a "do your own thing" ethos. The term free beat did not catch on, so for the purposes of this book, despite all the conceptual vagueness, it will remain krautrock.

Musicians such as Mani Neumeier (Guru Guru) and Jaki Liebezeit (Can) even found this free beat more attractive and, above all, freer than free jazz, in which both were successful as drummers. Liebezeit complained that in free jazz, strict rules on how to play were often replaced by prohibitions – what not to play under any circumstances. Free beat or psychedelic rock seemed to be much more open. It also offered more possibilities in terms of sound, especially through the use of electronic instruments, compared to free jazz, which essentially stuck to conventional jazz instruments. Just how close free jazz and psychedelic could be was demonstrated in particular by the English scene around groups such as AMM, who occasionally performed as a support act for Pink Floyd. Guitarist Derek Bailey called the concept non-idiomatic improvisation – improvised music whose vocabulary is no longer derived from the history of jazz or any other traditional music – Felix Klopotek coined the term "Niemandsmusik" (nobody's music) for it. Instead, the sounds of the European avant-garde found their way into the music. For the musicians, this opened up the possibility of stepping out of the epigonal position they had in relation to American jazz. This concept also became interesting for rock musicians who found themselves in a similar position. And it is still interesting for anyone who wants to break away from the predetermined musical paths that are largely inherent in both jazz and pop music.

There is hardly any criteria by which krautrock can be defined, unless you return the lowest common denominator: music from (West) Germany. That says nothing about the music. Instead, another category creeps in: individuality. As a translation of "do your own thing", the musicians would have agreed with this at the time. But in that case it would actually mean "their" thing and not the "German" thing. Because if the krautrockers wanted anything with their music, it was to put the greatest possible distance between themselves and the German nation. They wanted nothing more than to be part of the transnational musical movement that was first called beat and later rock. A label like krautrock, which defined a commonality according to national affiliation, which they did their utmost to conceal, was something they wanted to avoid at all costs. The term krautrock was also an invention of the British music magazine Melody Maker in the early 1970s and initially remained largely without consequence. Krautrock, with its relationship to the insult of "krauts" for Germans dating back to the First World War, was not necessarily meant as a compliment. Hans Joachim Irmler, keyboardist of Faust, tells the story like this: In response to the band's experience after relocating to England, where the less than friendly word "krauts" was still in use for Germans, the band had named a track "Krautrock" on the album *Faust IV*. The word would thus have come into the world in 1973. When the first records by Tangerine Dream or Amon Düül were made, nobody would have known what to do with the word. At best, people would have translated kraut as "weed" and thought of marijuana, which would not have been particularly far-fetched for this music.

The fact that decades later, attempts are being made to incorporate krautrock into a national identity cannot be blamed on the krautrockers, at least in the majority of cases; even if in recent years, some have opportunistically jumped on the bandwagon in order to put their faces in front of the camera for some documentary after years of being forgotten. Attempts to utilise krautrock for such projects have so far been largely unsuccessful. The music is obviously too unwieldy for that. The romantic anti-modernism echoed by some krautrock bands could also be a possible intersection for right-wing ideologies. However, as this anti-modernism was always associated with a wanderlust for North Africa, the Middle East or India and celebrated with exotic instruments, like sitars and flutes, it immediately eluded right-wing appropriation – to this day. Above all, the right doesn't need this convoluted music, especially in the present day. It has long since found a successful soundtrack in straight out rock, from Rammstein to Frei.Wild – the new German hardness. Though here the term rock should actually be written in inverted commas, as this music has harmonically and rhythmically whitewashed all traces of the African-American part of original rock and roll. To paraphrase Theweleit: body armour instead of swinging hips, death cult rather than life affirmation. Today's right-wingers would shout the same "with Adolf you all would have been ..." at the pot-smoking krautrockers clad in their Afghan coats, just like the diehards did back in the 1960s.

The fact that the term krautrock has long been met with a shrug of the shoulders in Germany, except among record collectors and a small fan community, is also due to the fact that the number of records produced in Germany between 1968 and 1974 is rather modest. Until a few years ago, it was always the same canon of just over a dozen bands – from A for Amon Düül to X for Xhol. Martin Büsser wrote in *testcard*: "Collectors may claim otherwise: Truly high-quality (...) Krautrock records can really only be counted on two hands. (...) The majority of what these bands later released lags behind their debuts to the point of embarrassment." Indeed, the most radical experiments can mainly be found on the debut albums. This is especially true in cases where conventional instruments, and traditional playing methods and forms, are set aside. Electronic sounds were the most effective means of breaking from conventions. It's no coincidence that the results were labelled "space music". A broad, mainly youthful audience had their first encounters with electronic sounds through soundtracks for science fiction films or radio plays.

If you were still too young to pack your bags and break free, there were still other options. Reading – but you had to figure that one out for yourself in a household without books. I took what I could get my hands on. At the age of twelve, I was immersed in stacks of science fiction pulp – the cheap magazine series that I bought second-hand because pocket money was tight. Or I could trade three books I'd already read for one I didn't know yet. My supply was provided by small shops, often in basements, which could be found on almost every street in the poorer neighbourhoods.

In the beginning, the publishers mainly brought out stories taken from the USA, which had already been published there in the 1940s. The translations were often rather uninspired, as I later realised when I read a few of the stories again in the original versions. The difference to the works by German authors was striking. German space was a thoroughly military affair. This can also be seen in the only sci-fi series produced for German television: Raumpatrouille Orion. Essentially, it was the relocation of the high command of the Wehrmacht into the infinite expanses of space (although women could also make a general's rank). In the beginning, the publishers of magazine series, such as Utopia, not only adopted the stories from the US: the covers were also taken from the originals. On the covers, good-looking space travellers and, above all, female space travellers, enticed the reader. However, the female astronauts, who were rather scantily clad despite the coldness of space, were not merely "damsels in distress" to be rescued by the hero. In many of these illustrations, female astronauts were piloting rockets, or teaching nasty aliens the meaning of fear with a ray gun in each hand. In contrast to this attractive cosmos, the covers of German stories were mostly without any women. Nor were there any men – just soldiers. Apparently the illustrators otherwise worked for the militaristic Landser series, which came from the same publisher.

COSMIC MUSIC

As early as the beginning of the 20th century, Arnold Schönberg wrote in the text to his Second String Quartet: "I feel air from another planet". The makers of science fiction films realised early on that not only the air on other planets had to be different, but also the music. Soundtracks such as that of *Forbidden Planet* (1956) were the cinema audience's first encounter with a purely electronic soundtrack (by Bebe and Louis Barron). One of the attractions of the 1958 World's Fair in Brussels was the pavilion designed by Le Corbusier and built by the electronics company Philips, in which Edgard Varèse's "Poème Électronique" was played from a surround system accompanied by a light show. This made electronic music known to a wide audience beyond the avant-garde circles. However, its production was still costly and only possible in a few suitably equipped studios. This changed in the mid 1960s with the first synthesisers being built in large numbers. 1967 then became the year of psychedelic space flights: The Rolling Stones travelled "2000 Light Years from Home", Jimi Hendrix viewed the "Third Stone from the Sun" from space, while Pink Floyd went into "Interstellar Overdrive". Cosmic was a favourite word in the Californian Summer of Love and Janis Joplin sang with the Kozmic Blues Band.

The term "Kosmische Musik" was in the air, but was mostly used by British fans in the German spelling specifically for krautrock. In Germany, the term first appeared on a series of records produced by Rolf-Ulrich Kaiser for his Kosmische

Kuriere label, which he founded in the early 1970s. He borrowed the name from Timothy Leary, with whom he had recorded the LP *Seven Up* after Leary had fled the USA. Later, the musicians involved in the Kosmische Kuriere sessions would complain that Kaiser had forced them to take LSD for the recordings. How much coercion was necessary, is left to the reader's imagination. Kaiser was initially an author (including *Protestfibel: Formen einer neuen Kultur* and *Underground? Pop? Nein! Gegenkultur!*), label manager (Ohr, Pilz) and producer, seen as one of the protagonists of the new German music scene. At some point he drifted into a parallel universe of belief, in the world-improving effects of mind-expanding drugs and tarot. Kaiser gradually lost control of his record company and disappeared from the public eye in the mid-1970s. The fact that he is remembered as a drug casualty does him an injustice. He was one of the first to propagate the developments of the American counterculture in Germany. However, he also warned early on against the same commercialisation that he was later accused of due to his collaboration with major record companies. Perhaps because of his balancing act between counterculture and commerce, he recognised earlier than others that counterculture was in danger of simply becoming one market segment among many.

AVANT-GARDE AND ELECTRONIC MUSIC

The term electronic music, as it emerged in the 1950s in the e-music avant-garde around the WDR Studio for Electronic Music, was expressly intended to be more than a mere description of the technical means of production. It was meant to be music that also broke new ground on a compositional level, only to be realised with electronic instruments. A distinction should therefore be made between electronic music and music with electronic instruments. Music with electronic instruments was neither new nor automatically avant-garde. In the USA, Raymond Scott was already recording advertising jingles in the early 1960s that used electronic sounds to emphasise the modernity of their products. He was one of the first to use a sequencer – for a series of records designed to put children to sleep with simple, repetitive patterns played with perfect timing: *Soothing Sounds for Baby*. As far back as in the 1930s, Oskar Sala had given concerts on the trautonium, an early synthesiser, impressing the Nazi propaganda minister Goebbels. Subsequently, the production of a "people's trautonium" was planned, because just as modern as the instrument was, the music Sala played on it was equally conventional. After the war, Sala recorded a number of film scores, from Edgar Wallace films such as *The Strangler of Blackmoor Castle* to Hitchcock's *The Birds*. The music for *The Birds* was indeed a novelty. Sala was a good craftsman who, where necessary, also sounded modern in his soundtracks to industrial films, like one for steel production at the firm Mannesmann. But he was rightly never regarded as an avant-garde composer.

In view of the musicians' later output, it is reasonable to suspect that some of the radical electronic experiments in early krautrock were not so much deliberately avant-garde as they were accidentally, because the new technology was not yet so easy to handle. The first synthesiser that could be bought in Europe and that was reasonably affordable did not have a normal keyboard, which forced musicians to explore other avenues. With the return of the keyboard, a tried and true tonality reemerged, which fell behind the level that the musical avant-garde had reached in the first half of the 20th century. For Kraftwerk, the arrival of electronic keyboards, on which nice melodies could once again be tinkled, signalled the end of radical experiments – at the same time, it was the beginning of their international success.

In pop discourse, both the group's free pieces and their songs – which were rather conventional except for their electronic instrumentation – are considered equally avant-garde. This raises the question of the criteria according to which this artistic seal of quality is awarded. The historical artistic avant-gardists of the 20th century were characterised by the fact that they not only wanted a change in art, but also a change in life. The most radical movements – Dada, the Situationists and Fluxus – also questioned the role of the artist as an individual genius. This was accompanied by a critique of the economic conditions of art and its production for a market. Another characteristic of the artistic avant-gardists of the 20th century were their manifestos, which expressed the intention to be more than just a new art movement or fashion. This claim can also be found with a number of krautrock bands, which means that the avant-garde label is potentially more suitable. The spectrum ranges from Ton Steine Scherben's manifesto "music is a weapon", in which music is more of a means to a (political) end, to Faust's manifesto inspired by the ideas of the Situationists. In the heated debates surrounding 1968, many of the krautrock bands took a political stance and saw not only their music, but above all, collective forms of life and production, as their contribution to changing society. In retrospect, this was simultaneously the most political and artistically creative period of krautrock. However, the great search and experimentation did not begin with krautrock. It had already begun earlier – in France with Pierre Schaeffer's musique concrète, in England with the work of the Radiophonic Workshop and in the experimental studios of German broadcasters, where composers such as Karlheinz Stockhausen worked.

KARLHEINZ STOCKHAUSEN

Karlheinz Stockhausen is often portrayed as a kind of godfather, and one sometimes has the impression that all krautrock musicians studied with him. In fact, there were only two: Irmin Schmidt and Holger Czukay, both from Can. The younger musicians, who had started out in beat bands, only became aware of Stockhausen when his photo appeared on the cover of *Sgt. Pepper's Lonely Hearts Club Band*. It took a detour via the Beatles to overcome the prejudice that the avant-garde was academic and hostile to pleasure. But then curiosity was aroused. The Swiss composer Thomas Kessler ran the Elektronik Beat Studio, set up by the West Berlin district of Wilmersdorf in the basement of a school in 1968, where young musicians could make recordings. Kessler took them to concerts by Iannis Xenakis and other avant-garde composers. For most of them, it was their first encounter with this music. Their curiosity was now aroused and they tried to merge these experiences with the rock music they had been making. Bands such as Tangerine Dream, Ash Ra Tempel and Agitation Free emerged from the scene that gathered around this studio, where they learnt to work with electronic sound generation and tape manipulation.

In the 1960s, few people embodied the musical avant-garde as intensely as Karlheinz Stockhausen. He was born in 1928, and his mother was murdered by the National Socialists in 1941 as part of the euthanasia programme. His father was killed in action, and the 16-year-old had to care for dying soldiers in a military hospital.

These were traumatic experiences for a teenager. Karlheinz Stockhausen processed them musically in "Michaels Jugend", a section from his 30-hour opera cycle *Licht – Die 7 Tage der Woche*. It was commissioned by Recha Freier, lyricist and organiser of the Testimonium concert series in Jerusalem. In 1933 Freier was one of the founders of the Youth Aliyah, an organisation that helped Jewish children emigrate to Palestine, thus saving them from the Nazi extermination camps. She managed to escape from Nazi Germany in 1941. The composition commission turned into a friendship between Stockhausen and Freier, and "Michaels Jugend" was premiered in Israel in 1979.

After the war, Stockhausen studied in Paris with Olivier Messiaen. There, he familiarised himself with the techniques of musique concrète, and from 1953 he was an assistant at the WDR Studio for Electronic Music founded by Herbert Eimert, which he later took over as director. Stockhausen was influential not only as a composer, but also as a theorist and as one of the leading figures of the Darmstadt Summer Courses for New Music. Stockhausen also had qualities as a charismatic self-promoter, which gave him a pop appeal and made his already conflict-ridden relationship with the conservative music world even more difficult. In the 1950s, pre-1945 personnel were still employed there and felt that they were the guardians of German cultural superiority. Stockhausen's popularity as a radical innovator reached a peak at the 1970 World Exhibition in Osaka, where he performed for a number of weeks in front of a large audience in a spherical auditorium with movable loudspeakers. Despite the great success, there was the usual behind the scenes wrangling between traditionalists and modernists – so fierce that for a while Stockhausen wanted to leave the project.

Stockhausen made few or no political statements. The political was in his music, as was shown at a concert in West Berlin. In 1963, two compositions by Karlheinz Stockhausen – "Refrain" and "Kontakte" – were performed in the newly built Congress Hall under the motto "Music in the Technical Age". During the interval between the two pieces, a conversation took place between the music critic Hans Heinz Stuckenschmidt and Karlheinz Stockhausen. Stockhausen explained the structure of "Refrain": "As you have noticed yourself, the basic measure for these three musicians in "Refrain" is not a time signature, a time (...) to be filled with sound, but that a sound time animates this piece." Stockhausen provided the following instructions for the musicians: when a "sound has diminished by a certain degree of intensity, then someone else will play to their tone. And there is a constant change in whoever of the three musicians has the floor – or we say: whoever sets the tone. This is literally true here. They set the tone one after the other – without anything like a conductor – which we have experienced for quite a long time." At this point, a loud murmur goes through the audience. 1963 – the end of the Third Reich was only 18 years earlier. The audience sitting in the West Berlin Congress Hall still knew exactly who and what was meant by "the one who sets the tone".

The spherical auditorium in Osaka with its multi-channel technology, image, and film feeds would have been the dream of many a krautrocker. Faust tried something similar at their first concert, which ended in a fiasco because the technology failed, but also because the band couldn't live up to the hype that their manager Uwe Nettelbeck had generated. With Can, Holger Czukay made the most consistent use of the tape manipulation techniques learnt from Stockhausen, and the use of "non-musical" noises.

Perhaps even more influential upon the krautrockers than Karlheinz Stockhausen was the American avant-garde scene consisting of Steve Reich, Philip Glass, Terry Riley and Tony Conrad – the protagonists of minimal music. Tony Conrad, who also played with Faust, was more of a special case with his endless microtonal drones on bowed instruments, which created a complex harmony beyond the equal-tempered tuning, but in the longer term he was certainly the most interesting and radical. The repetitive patterns of Reich and Glass had more of an influence on krautrock. Their music was considerably more accessible and easier to follow. The instrumentation was also largely what was available in a rock band anyway. Most krautrock bands played comparatively cheap organs from Italy, which are still popular with garage bands today. They characterised the sound of early recordings by Can, Cluster and Tangerine Dream, and could easily be altered with any of the effects devices that were originally developed for electric guitars. Reverb and echo devices were used excessively, as they created artificial spaces and a feeling of vastness that was lacking in everyday life.

What united the discourses in the ranks of new music composers with many krautrock musicians and free jazz protagonists, was the feeling of being at a ground zero. But it was not only the old musical certainties that were called into question. It also applied to the society from which they had emerged. Nothing was certain anymore: everything could be, and had to be, questioned. For musicians, this also meant asking the question of what music is, and when sound becomes music.

What made the relationship with the established avant-garde difficult was its tendency towards academia. A flyer for the band Eruption, founded by Conrad Schnitzler in 1971, put it more simply: "Eruption gets the prisoners out of their ivory towers. (...) Eruption will send sounds into the room from all directions. (...) Eruption shows the basic processes of new music. Eruption proves that there are no secret devices. Eruption shows that the player is simultaneously instrument maker, performer and composer." Probably the greatest merit of the krautrock bands, at least the most musically radical ones at the beginning such as Kluster, Tangerine Dream or Faust, is that they liberated the ideas discussed in the musical avant-garde from their academic ghetto, and removed the aura of genius that was only bestowed upon a select few. It was the spirit of the Fluxus happenings, which combined visual art, performance, and music, and sought to liberate them from the academic and the solemn atmosphere of the art temples. Art should be social action and not a dead museum piece.

THE SOUND OF KRAUT – THE RUHR REGION

Where did the first krautrock band come from? From the USA. They were The Monks, five American GIs who were stationed in a garrison near Frankfurt, and stayed in West Germany after their service ended. There, they toured the clubs playing rock and roll as The 5 Torkays. Until they met two budding designers in 1965 – Karl-H. Remy, a student at the Ulm School of Design, and Walther Niemann, a student at the Folkwang School in Essen. Both studied at universities that were committed to the design principles of Bauhaus. With them, the musicians created a new sound and a new image. From then on, the band was called The Monks. The music was simplified and underpinned by a motoric beat. The Monks disbanded and were long forgotten until 1980, when the records were rediscovered with punk and Neue Deutsche Welle (new German wave). If the two designers had disguised the band as robots instead of the monkish image, they might have gone down in history as Kraftwerk's role models instead of punk precursors.

The range of krautrock between progressive rock, world music and abstract electronics, is also a result of the different social backgrounds of the musicians, and the differences between the war generation and those born in the post-war period. Regional differences also played a role. These included who lived in which occupation zone, and therefore which of the radio programmes broadcast for the Allied soldiers they could tune in to. The industrial heart of the old Federal Republic lay between Düsseldorf, Cologne and Wuppertal. The Ruhr area had experienced several waves of immigration: Poles before the Second World War, displaced persons afterwards, and then guest workers from southern Europe and Turkey. It was a hard-labour culture characterised by work in collieries and steelworks. People had to be able to rely on each other beneath the ground. Competition could be fatal. This continued above ground in the settlements, where everyone built houses together. There is a great similarity to the English industrial cities here, so it is no wonder that the British Invasion – The Beatles, The Who, The Kinks – triggered a wave of beat bands forming in the Ruhr area. In addition to this rather proletarian movement, there was the influence of the art academies. The cities had money and spent it on culture. Wuppertal became one of the birthplaces of free jazz with Peter Brötzmann and Peter Kowald as central figures. In Cologne, Can was founded in the scene around WDR broadcasting and its electronics studio. In

Düsseldorf, the Art Academy became a point of reference for Kraftwerk and Neu!.

Düsseldorf, Cologne and Wuppertal, with their westwards-orientated art scene, were closest to the developments of Pop Art in England and the USA, which also influenced the music scene. The Velvet Underground, who were the antithesis of the "peace and love" of the hippies that dominated at the end of the 1960s, were known here early on through their connection to Andy Warhol. In 1963, the painters Gerhard Richter, Sigmar Polke and Konrad Lueg organised an exhibition entitled *Living with Pop – A Demonstration for Capitalist Realism*. It was an installation in a furniture store in which the artists took part as living exhibits. The inspiration came from American and British pop culture, although the organisers were aware that Germany was lagging behind both artistic and social developments. They deliberately chose a furniture store that did not offer modern designer furniture, as one would have expected under the keyword "pop". The product range of the Berges company, in whose premises the action took place, catered to the petty-bourgeois, stuffy taste of German post-war living rooms. This contradiction between transnational modernity and the relics of a German identity can also be found on Kraftwerk's album covers.

The Zero group was founded in Düsseldorf in 1958 around the painters Heinz Mack, Otto Piene and Gunther Uecker. The explanation for the name was to start from a ground zero, from which to orientate oneself without historical ballast. This zero point was intended to be positive and optimistic. This is most evident in Heinz Mack's light sculptures. However, they also show that even if one wants to be free from historical ballast, it could not be done without role models. Mack's works are reminiscent of the "Raum Licht Modulator" by Bauhaus artist Láslό

Moholy-Nagy, whose films such as *Lichtspiel Schwarz Weiss Grau* from 1930 also became a model for Conrad Schnitzler's video works. The influence of Bauhaus aesthetics also had a musical impact on groups such as Kraftwerk, which were founded in the context of the Düsseldorf art scene.

At the southern end of the Ruhr region lies Cologne, where the band Can was formed in 1968 by the two Stockhausen students – Irmin Schmidt and Holger Czukay. The two deliberately chose musicians with different musical backgrounds in order to escape academic music. They found them in Jaki Liebezeit, who played drums in Manfred Schoof's free jazz band, and guitarist Michael Karoli, who was a few years younger and had a background in rock music. Cologne is also the headquarters of WDR, Germany's largest regional public broadcaster. This proximity helped the band to receive a number of commissions for film music. This included the soundtrack for one of the then-successful TV thrillers by British author Francis Durbridge, which, unusually for krautrock, gave the band a hit. However, WDR was particularly important because of its studio for electronic music, where Karlheinz Stockhausen, Gottfried Michael Koenig and Franco Evangelisti worked. The Gruppo di Improvvisazione Nuova Consonanza, founded by Franco Evangelisti in Italy, became one of the first music groups to make improvised music based not on free jazz, but instead on new music. After Stockhausen took over the leadership of the studio, he endeavoured to make every sound musically usable. In his composition "Mikrophonie", several musicians work on a large gong with metal parts or timpani mallets, while Stockhausen processes the result captured by microphones live through filters. The working methods developed in this way in the WDR studio, then found their way out of academic circles and into pop music via musicians such as Schmidt and Czukay. This pleasantly distinguished Can from the romantic, civilisation-weary longing for some imagined pre-modern world that was common among many krautrockers, standing in strange contrast to their preference for the latest electronic music. The cover of Can's *Ege Bamyasi* album looks different. As a humorous adaptation of Warhol's Campbell Soup can, a tin of okra from the Turkish grocer around the corner is depicted. The intrusion of social reality entered the otherwise escapist krautrock which had largely ignored Germany's transformation into a country of immigration. Perhaps because the actual migrants were labourers and not characters from Karl May's fictional journeys to the Orient.

FRANKFURT

It is difficult to name a krautrock band associated with Frankfurt. In Wiesbaden, not far away, there was Xhol Caravan, who later shortened their name to Xhol. Frankfurt was the centre of the German jazz scene in the 1950s, with the Mangelsdorff brothers being its most famous names. Their enthusiasm for jazz began during the Nazi era, when a group of the Swingjugend (Swing Youth) in Frankfurt used to meet in a Hot Club to listen to forbidden jazz. After the war, the conditions for jazz musicians were favourable, as Frankfurt was home to the headquarters of the US Army and there were plenty of opportunities to play jazz in the GI clubs. At the beginning, the most important part of the arrangement was a good meal and American cigarettes. There was also the opportunity to play with American musicians. The trombonist Albert Mangelsdorff, the younger of the two brothers, became an advocate of the emerging free jazz in the 1960s, facing hostility from the traditionalists.

At the end of the 1960s, the group Just Music led by saxophonist Alfred Harth operated in the border area between jazz and improvised music, which was more influenced by John Cage. Alfred Harth was also one of the musicians whose path ran parallel between music and the visual arts. The fact that this group never found its way into the krautrock canon is not only due to its proximity to jazz. As we see with musicians like Wolfgang Dauner, genre boundaries were quite permeable back then. What makes today's image of krautrock so unobjective is the fact that only what is available on record goes down in history. Recordings, especially of a professional standard, were still the exception at the end of the 1960s. Therefore, only a small part of the actual musical output of the time is accessible. The focus shifted once again with TV documentaries. Here, the only criteria was the existence of footage, which is why you always see the same film snippets in dozens of these documentaries.

This imbalance applies, for example, to the jam sessions in Heidi Loves You, of which no footage exists. The author Paul Gerhard Hübsch (later Hadayatullah Hübsch) founded this head shop in 1968 as a psychedelic centre and meeting place, deliberately distancing himself from the scene around the Frankfurt SDS (Socialist German Student Association), which was considered too intellectual. Frankfurt's contribution to the underground or counterculture of these years was more of a literary nature. The satirical magazine *Pardon*, one of the most important publications of the emerging left-wing spectrum, was published there. In its best year, the magazine, which was regularly criticised by conservatives, especially Franz Josef Strauß, sold over 300,000 copies. Also based in Frankfurt was März Verlag, which promoted American underground literature in Germany with its anthology *Acid*, edited by Rolf Dieter Brinkmann and Ralf-Rainer Rygulla. One of the popular titles, not only among literature enthusiasts but also among students and apprentices, was the book *Sexfront* by Günther Amendt, a polemic against repressive sexual morality. This group of readers also reached for the *Headcomix* by American comic artist Robert Crumb, published by März. The Crumb stories were translated by Bernd Brummbär, who, motivated by their success, founded his own underground magazine, *Germania*, which also contained the first articles about krautrock bands.

HAMBURG

The Hamburg bands with the legacy of the Starclub and the Liverpool connection came closest to the original British beat music, and therefore sounded the least like krautrock. From Hamburg came The Rattles, who had performed at the Starclub together with The Beatles, as well as Wonderland, Les Humphries Singers, Atlantis and Frumpy. That was all mainstream rock. Much more radical was the Hamburg film scene, where the Hamburg Film Cooperative was founded in 1968 around Hellmuth Costard, Werner Nekes and Barbara Riek as an answer to the underground films coming from the USA and Great Britain. In contrast to the Berlin DFFB, where politically unambiguous agitation films were propagated at the end of the 1960s, the Hamburg Cooperative was more interested in aesthetic experimentation and film as an experimental process, working mostly with simple technical means: a hand-held camera, cheap Super 8 film and without the usual complexities of film. The Co-op filmmakers wanted to distance themselves from conventional film and its production methods. A film by Hellmuth Costard became a scandal at the Oberhausen Short Film Festival in 1968, the title of which bore the label used by the state film subsidy board for its assessment of films with particular merit: *Besonders wertvoll*. Costard shows a close-up of his penis "lip-synching" the speech on film funding by a CDU member of parliament. There was an uproar because the festival did not want to show the film. In the cultural section of the newspaper *Die Zeit*, film critic Uwe Nettelbeck defended Costard's film and praised it as a radical work of art that was uncompromising, and therefore could not be marketed. This partisanship was not the only reason why Nettelbeck lost his job. After an intermezzo as editor-in-chief of the magazine *Konkret*, where he fell out with Ulrike Meinhof, Nettelbeck was unemployed. Polydor, whose management wanted to tap into the short-lived krautrock hype, approached Nettelbeck and asked if he knew a band that could fill this gap in the label's catalogue. Nettelbeck asked for an advance and set off in search for a suitable act in the scene around the Hamburg Film Cooperative and the Academy of Art. He found two bands, from whose union a group emerged that was christened Faust. The band used the advance to set up a studio in a small town between Hamburg and Bremen. The radical aesthetic, which was characterised by the band's connections to the work of Film Co-op and the visual arts, provided the necessary distance from the Hamburg rock scene and the musical mainstream, and made Faust one of the most interesting and enduringly influential bands of the krautrock scene.

Montage and collage were familiar working methods in film, but such an approach was unusual for bands. The Beatles were among the first pop musicians to venture into this area, but still remained rooted in conventional song structures. It apparently took people like Faust, who had not gone through the school of years of playing rock or jazz standards, to cross this boundary.

When sound film was introduced, there was a debate about how to deal with the new medium, and the Soviet filmmakers around, Eisenstein and Vertov in particular, argued that the potential of the new technology would be wasted if sound was only used to illustrate what was already visible. In this tradition, Faust provided the soundtrack to cinema in the mind. Until then, such musical strategies had only existed in the academic avant-garde. Just like Conrad Schnitzler, Faust tore the veil of exclusivity from electronic music. They did the same with Frank Zappa, whose influence is unmistakable, especially on the band's second album. Faust audibly adapted US garage rock with a good dose of irony, but one can also hear that they loved it. Their lyrics were laconic and refused to "make sense" superficially. The band obviously realised that their knowledge of English was not sufficient for lyrical excellence. Faust made a virtue of necessity and limited themselves to a few lines in the tradition of Dada and Kurt Schwitters. In the town of Wümme, a bridge was built between krautrock and the US avant-garde. In Germany, this was mostly only known from records. And this knowledge was also limited to small art circles, including Uwe Nettelbeck, Faust's manager. Tony Conrad was primarily known there as a filmmaker. In the 1960s, Conrad played the violin in the Theatre of Eternal Music founded by La Monte Young in New York – also known as The Dream Syndicate (with John Cale, among others, who joined the Velvet Underground shortly afterwards). With the microtonal drones of his violin, Conrad created a much more radical form of minimal music than the often rather sweet arpeggios of Steve Reich. The recordings were never released due to internal disputes within the group. In 1972, Conrad was in Germany for a screening of his films, and was invited by Uwe Nettelbeck to Wümme to record in Faust's studio. It would certainly have been difficult to realise Conrad's musical ideas with the complete Faust line-up. The sessions were limited to bass and drums most of the time, so that Tony Conrad's hypnotic violin dominates the atmosphere. It was also necessary for Conrad to intervene with the Faust musicians, who simply had anarchic fun playing: less, less – even less. The record was released in 1973 under a title that was an allusion to the Dream Syndicate recordings, which were kept under lock and key by La Monte Young: *Outside the Dream Syndicate*. The complete remixed sessions are now available.

MUNICH

Another centre of krautrock was Munich, with Amon Düül I + II, Popol Vuh and Embryo. The esoteric and life-reforming groups that were already strong in Munich in the first half of the 20th century also seem to have rubbed off on the music – be it the world music of Embryo, the archaic music of Amon Düül (before their schism) or the pseudo-religious music of Popol Vuh. The most radical notion was the concept of Amon Düül I: a commune in which everyone, adults and children, played music together. As radical as the idea was, the result was questionable. Instead of using the declared freedom to explore new musical territory, they stuck to the lowest common denominator of endless drumming, as can still be heard today at any stoner gathering in the park during summer.

For the musicians in the group, being held back in their musical ambitions by the collective claim was frustrating in the long run, which led to the split and the formation of Amon Düül II. The most interesting musical result was the album Phallus Dei, which lies between the two poles of collective freak-out and experienced rock band.

EVERYWHERE & NOWHERE

One cliché associated with krautrock is that of the rural commune making music together. The slogan "Aus grauer Städte Mauern" ("out of grey city walls") was already popular among young people in the scouting and hiking movements in the 1920s. From around 1970, moving to the countryside also appeared to be a suitable strategy for musicians to solve several problems at once: saying goodbye to the bourgeois nuclear family and joining a collective based on solidarity, from which they hoped to heal all their psychological wounds – only to have the same four faces sitting at the table of the rural commune for months on end, while the rain poured down outside. They hoped to have plenty of time for musical self-discovery, along with a rehearsal room that could be used around the clock, and whose noise emissions would at most disturb the cows in the surrounding pastures. However, this could also lead to the question of who was doing the washing up, and the discussion about who made a mistake while playing music becoming an unresolvable tangle. The only escape remaining was the one village pub to be found far and wide. Nevertheless, such problems could also be productive, as Ulf Meifert reports on life in Faust's quarters: "We were definitely political in the sense that everything should be done by everyone, in art and life (...). This was expressed in the fact that there were no designated composers of individual pieces or any stars. Here we were a real group, where it was clear that the person who did the washing up for two whole days was just as involved in the more or less ingenious ideas that were being realised in the studio as the proverbial housewife was in her husband's career." In the case of the most radical left-wing band, Ton Steine Scherben, of all people, authorship remained a matter of private appropriation, which led to endless legal disputes in the still seemingly distant future.

However, you first had to be able to afford the cheap country life. The infrastructure of the cities, from which one was now cut off, always offered the opportunity to earn a few Deutschmarks somewhere, especially in times of the so-called economic miracle. This was particularly important for those who had no family backing them to help out either regularly or at least in emergencies. There were plenty of empty farms in remote areas that you could move into for minimal rent, but you couldn't have any particular expectations of comfort. The winters in particular were not exactly what Californian hippie dreams were made of. Job opportunities were rare in the increasingly depopulated rural solitude. The farms were so cheap because everyone wanted to leave. How many bands went down this path and how much perseverance they had in doing so is not documented anywhere, just as no one knows how many bands even existed that fit the already very vague criteria of krautrock. Anyone who didn't leave behind at least one record for collectors' markets and reissues, is just as forgotten as the hundreds of beat bands that had emerged a few years earlier.

WEST BERLIN

Even further away from the urban and cultural centres in the west of the republic, right in the middle of the GDR, lay West Berlin, artificially kept alive as a "showcase of the free West" through subsidies. The most effective measure to attract young people to West Berlin was not the merit of political decisions made by German governments. Rather, it was West Berlin's status as a special case that remained under Allied administration, and the fact that it was still subject to the 1946 Control Council Law on the Dissolution of the Wehrmacht. As a result, the Bundeswehr had no presence in West Berlin, and West Berliners were exempt from compulsory military service, which was reintroduced in 1956 amid great resistance. Those who wanted to avoid conscription enrolled at one of West Berlin's universities. It was more complicated for young workers to avoid compulsory military service, although thanks to having their own income, the question of how they would support themselves was not a problem. Compulsory military service began at the age of 18. However, until 1975, one only became of legal age at 21, and thereby also fully independent in choosing where to live. It was legally possible to refuse to do military service, but the commissions responsible for recognising conscientious objectors, which remained the required means until 1976, were largely made up of old Nazis, for whom every objector was a deserter and potential traitor to the country. For young workers, who could not argue as eloquently as their middle class peers, this oral hearing was an even greater hurdle.

Even though West Berlin was quite cut off from the rest of the Federal Republic and could only be reached via transit routes, it produced its own krautrock scene. One centre was the Zodiak Free Arts Lab, founded by Conrad Schnitzler in 1968. Schnitzler was born in Düsseldorf in 1937. Towards the end of the war, he made his way on foot to Austria, where his mother had already been evacuated. What characterised Schnitzler, and other musicians who had grown up in the final years of the war and experienced how order only slowly stabilised in the post-war years, was a great deal of independence. And a sense of practicality – you had to develop this in the period immediately after the war in order to get by. They also had a deep-seated mistrust of authority, as they had seen the heroes of their childhood turn out to be criminals in 1945. In Austria, Schnitzler was sent to the village school with all children, regardless of age. The main thing was to keep them off the streets. After the war, he completed a mechanical engineering apprenticeship and then went to sea to avoid conscription. When he heard that there was a professor at the Düsseldorf Art Academy who would accept anyone into his class, even if they didn't have A-levels, he began studying sculpture with Joseph Beuys. In 1961, Schnitzler and his young family moved to West Berlin, lured by the benefits the city offered to immigrants.

In Wolfgang Müller's book Subkultur Westberlin 1979–1989, *which covers the time when krautrock was already history and largely forgotten in Germany, there is a map of the locations you had to have been to in order to belong. The addresses roughly coincide with the route of the number 19 bus, the only one that ran all night each quarter of an hour between Kurfürstendamm and Hermannplatz, where Kreuzberg and Neukölln meet. Until 1989, it remained the lifeline of West Berlin's subculture for anyone who couldn't afford a taxi. The Zodiak Free Arts Lab was located under the Schaubühne theatre, within walking distance of the number 19 night bus, in the area on Hallesches Ufer that was still dominated by war ruins. A rather colourful mix gathered there – from art students to young workers. Young workers is not quite accurate – young no-longer-workers would have been the more appropriate term. The art students came to Zodiak because Conrad Schnitzler, who initiated the club, was part of the Berlin Fluxus scene. The (no-longer) workers came because the club was in Kreuzberg, where many of them lived. Both groups were united by a left-wing identity, but there were certainly differences. While the predominantly student left tended to discuss anti-colonialism or the Vietnam War in the abstract, the opposition of young workers was much more determined by their own daily experience of repression at home, at school and at work. I had already met some of them at the Stones concert at the Waldbühne, which had mysteriously turned out to be a kind of initiation. In retrospect, it's pretty amazing what we projected onto music back then. As this scene became more and more radicalised, it initially called itself "The Blues" until it became the "Rambling Hash Rebels" and later the "June 2 Movement".*

One of the ongoing conflicts with the state was over the consumption of hashish. This also eventually led to the closure of the Zodiak. In its short existence, however, the place offered a programme that opened a door for me. When I was 16 I began playing in one of the many school bands, on drums – which initially meant a snare drum and a cardboard box for a bass drum. That didn't matter. It was still great fun for band members and party guests alike. The audience danced – and that was what it was all about. The era of these bands, fuelled more by enthusiasm than musical expertise, came to an end in the late 1960s and I swapped my cheap drum kit for a holiday in the south of France to enjoy the end of my school days. My beat band "career" was over, but my enthusiasm for music was still there, even if it seemed to be limited to hours of listening to records while stoned. The hippest bands of the Berlin scene played at Zodiak. For example, Tangerine Dream, who were still playing psychedelic rock with endless guitar solos. It was still close to the music I had known up to that point. But there was also a completely new with the groups around Conrad Schnitzler and Hans-Joachim Roedelius, who played under different names such as Plus Minus, Human Being, Eruption, Kluster or Geräusche. The musical programme was also titled Geräusche: any sound could become part of the performance. Before Faust (and at least a decade before Einstürzende Neubauten), hammers and saws became musical instruments. What was all that about? I had never heard the name John Cage before. Or Fluxus.

After I got involved in the Zodiak scene and became friends with Conrad Schnitzler, everything took place very quickly. Two things happened, the chronology of which can only be reconstructed to a limited extent. Schnitzler always regarded his groups as open experimental arrangements, where he explored in changing constellations. Schnitzler had no interest in a band as a fixed formation, which made it easy to make a connection. The fact that I no longer had an instrument wasn't a problem either. You just had to find something that made noise. At the same time, someone from the Zodiak scene introduced me to a young musician who wanted to put together a band for a theatre group: Ralph Möbius, who later became known under his stage name Rio Reiser. There was an old drum kit lying around in the theatre group's rooms and so we started playing as a trio – bass, guitar and drums. Most of the time we played endless improvisations, fuelled in equal parts by riffs borrowed from the Stones and drugs that were always around, even when the fridge was empty. Directly in parallel with Ton Steine Scherben *becoming a real band with real songs, the fun diminished in equal measure. After two years and one LP, Scherben issued a press release saying that I was leaving the group to join Eruption, the group of Klaus Freudigmann and Conrad Schnitzler.*

In the early 60s, most of the clubs or back rooms of pubs where you could listen to rock and roll and beat were in the proletarian, working class districts of the city. The musicians in the bands came from the same milieu as their audience. The bands' repertoires consisted of cover versions. It wasn't about art. None of the musicians – all of them amateurs – saw themselves as artists. It was all about having fun on the weekend, dancing and flirting. If you enter "Saturday" in the search field on Discogs, you get more than 90,000 hits. The musicians who became professionals played every weekend and more, and could earn the same income as a skilled labourer, but usually they realistically saw it as a transitory biographical stage. Hardly anyone could imagine growing old as a beat musician. As pop music became increasingly sophisticated, both musically and in terms of recording technology, many of the venues were converted into discotheques that could react quickly to changing public tastes. The bands from the first half of the 60s, whose proof of success was the number of dancers on the dance floor, disappeared. There was a generational shift, which also changed the social composition of the bands. The children of the middle classes saw themselves much more as artists and saw their music less as a mixture of fun and service, and more as a strategy for self-realisation. The children of the bourgeoisie were consciously anti-bourgeois. It was a cocktail of bohemian clichés and undigested left-wing ideology that produced strange blossoms, as you can read in an early Tangerine Dream interview that appeared in *Linkeck*, one of West Berlin's numerous underground magazines, from 1968. Tangerine Dream are introduced like this:

The Tangerine Dreams are likely the only free-beat band in West Germany (comparable to Pink Floyd).
  L: You wouldn't make a beat to dance to?
  TD: No, definitely not. We are no longer prepared to work with people who only want to exploit us for certain purposes and who don't care about our music, even if there is a lot of money in it.
  L: What do you do for a living?
  TD: All of us used to work, were terribly well-behaved and industrious, some of us studied. The singer was in a financial position where he never needed to do anything. Volker, the saxophonist, is studying film technology in Berlin and will finish in the summer. The drummer used to work, he also has an apprenticeship behind him, at some point it sparked. I don't know, perhaps it has also happened to you – that at some point you realise the pointlessness of work, that you can no longer cling to it and try to shape your life the way you want to. With the consequence that you no longer do anything.

Which is something that you have to be able to afford. You certainly didn't earn anything from the concerts organised by the "Central Council of Rambling Hash Rebels" in the old canteen of the Technical University. The posters depicted bands like Ashra Tempel and Agitation Free in a comic book style, with huge joints, machine guns and slogans like "Frei sein, high sein, Terror muss dabei sein" (be free, be high, terror must be part of it). Bands who asked for a fee were suspected of being on a capitalist trip. The income from ticket sales was low anyway due to the cheap ticket prices. And whatever was in the till became a solidarity contribution to "comrades in prison" or "liberation movements".

Earning money with art in West Berlin was difficult, as there was largely no wealthy, art-orientated middle class. Earning money with music in West Berlin was even more difficult, as there was no surrounding area where bands could have played. Travelling throughout West Germany meant travelling at least 300 kilometres on the transit routes through the GDR. Before the treaties with the GDR were enforced, the border controls were a real horror trip. The GDR border guards unrestrainedly took out their German resentment against anything non-conformist on the long-haired musicians. They were then allowed to spend hours unscrewing all the loudspeaker boxes to ensure that no refugees or smuggled goods were concealed inside. People thought three times about venturing out on such trips, especially as the arrival points on the western side, Helmstedt or Marienborn, were still far away from the centres of the Federal Republic. There still wasn't a motorway to Hamburg. The country road that led there went through a Soviet army training area, where you could expect an unlit tank to suddenly appear across the carriageway.

One consequence of West Berlin's peripheral location, and the very limited number of performance opportunities in the city, was that no major jazz scene developed in West Berlin. There were one or two clubs where modern jazz was played, which no longer sounded so modern towards the end of the 1960s. Anyone who was serious about being a jazz musician packed their bags and went out into West Germany. The free jazz musicians fared a little better – in other words, just as badly as everywhere else. At least they had the advantage of being up-to-date and, thanks to their proximity to the visual arts and the associated institutions, had other opportunities to perform at galleries or art events outside the normal music scene. The Zodiak became a venue for this scene. Its proximity to the theatre alone suggested concepts beyond the usual concert format with the separation between stage and audience. The first performances by Kluster (renamed Cluster in 1971) took place in galleries, and the first solo albums by Conrad Schitzler were produced in René Block's gallery. Other galleries and subsidised art events were also important, especially those of the Akademie der Künste.

The West Berlin krautrock scene was only slightly influenced by jazz, but all the more by the younger musicians coming from beat music. Consequently, bands like Ash Ra Tempel or Agitation Free had much more of a rock sound. Tangerine Dream occupied the middle ground. Founder Edgar Froese had studied painting and graphics at the West Berlin University of the Arts. When he played at Zodiak for the first time, his band was still a psychedelic rock band, playing a blend of the Velvet Underground and early Syd Barrett-era Pink Floyd. It then shrunk to a trio with Klaus Schulze, on the trail of Cream's endless guitar solos. The collaboration with Schnitzler set a decisive course for the future. The first LP *Electronic Meditation* is a free sound collage, sounding more like Schnitzler's groups Geräusche or Kluster than what Tangerine Dream had done before. Even though Schnitzler, who found a permanent band too restrictive, left after this LP, it was something of a big bang for Tangerine Dream. What they soon lost once again, however, was Schnitzler's fearless embrace of noise and dissonance.

Much of the music from West Berlin had a dark quality, which is not surprising in the shadow of the Wall. In the accompanying text of a CD with archive material from the time when Conrad Schnitzler parted ways with Hans-Joachim Roedelius and Dieter Moebius (there was some lingering confusion about the band names Kluster and Eruption), the mood of the city is described as "Black Spring" – the long, cold winters in laboriously heated flats, and an air filled with the smell of sulphur from the brown coal burned in East Berlin, which first turned the snow brown, then black. Perhaps that explains the difference to the scene in the Rhineland and Munich. But life was cheap and West Berlin's subsidised economy allowed some of the money that was channelled into the city to trickle down as well.

NOISE AND INFINITE SPACES

At the heart of Kluster's sound was Schnitzler's conviction, taken from John Cage, that every sound can be used musically. While guitarists dreamed of the same guitar that Hendrix played, Schnitzler had glass balls spinning in a metal bowl. Instead of saving up for Hendrix's wah-wah pedal, he experimented with cheap contact microphones that were glued to anything that could be hit, stroked, scratched or shaken. The poor sound quality of these microphones, which were otherwise used in telephones, provided a welcomed alienating effect. One of the few means of sound manipulation available at the time had an almost programmatic effect: artificial reverberation and endless echoes catapulted the music into strange spaces, which, in contrast to the cramped gloom of German living rooms filled with huge, intimidating furniture, sent the listener into infinite expanses. This reflected the mood of the generation who, as soon as they had their own flat, got rid of this ballast and reduced their furnishings to a mattress and a bookshelf, (not just out of economic necessity). And – very importantly – a stereo system.

Reverb, echo, distortion, and wah-wah pedals were the only electronic instruments at the beginning. Only ring modulators, which were relatively easy to build, and frequency generators that had been repurposed from measurement technology, found their way into the music of Can, Kluster and Kraftwerk early on. In order to break new ground, it was often enough to push existing instruments against the grain. During his time with Tangerine Dream, which is documented on the first LP Electronic Meditation, Schnitzler played a cello stripped of all euphony by the effects devices he used and with objects shoved between the strings. He sat with his back to the audience, an electric guitar on his knees, which was abused with bits of metal. However, Schnitzler did not invent this technique. The debate as to where the boundary between noise and musical sound lies had been discussed among avant-garde composers for some time. They were interested in breaking free from the constraints of the established sounds within the orchestral instrumentarium, which were laden with formulated meaning. Schnitzler also had early contact with the British improvised music scene, where musicians, such as Derek Bailey and groups such as AMM, had been experimenting with these playing techniques for some time.

SYNTHETIC MUSIC

The synthesiser is regarded as the sonic hallmark of krautrock. But most of the records that define the genre were created without it, as these instruments were scarcely available at the end of the 1960s. The electronic organ was an intermediate stage and the first instrument in the krautrock toolbox to earn the adjective electronic. In the form of the Hammond organ, this instrument had already been established for a while and, despite its relatively short history, was already steeped in tradition thanks to its use in jazz. It turned out to be a stroke of luck that a real Hammond organ was astronomically expensive in Europe, and a nightmare to lug around to concerts – especially if you played it through a Leslie cabinet, which was essential for the "proper" sound. For a touring beat band, there was a cheaper and more transportable alternative – the so-called combo organ, primarily made in Italy (in fact, the Italian contribution to the pop and psychedelic music of the 1960s is often overlooked). Instead of the full, gospel choir-invoking sound of the Hammond organ, this instrument had a rather cold timbre that was without associations from any tradition (this sound has since become the cliché for sixties-heavy garage rock). Kraftwerk's decision to use such an instrument was certainly not the result of an anorexic piggy bank. Florian Schneider's father was a successful architect, a representative of the International style, which propagated an architecture freed from all traditions and the ballast of regional identity. The tradition-free sound of the combo organ fulfilled the same function musically. The departure from regionalism and identity kitsch became Kraftwerk's recipe for success, even if they flirted with their Germanness on the level of their constructed image. More precisely: Kraftwerk played with the contradiction between identity and modernity. The German identity only came across as a shadow of the past, as a kind of wistful childhood memory of Christmas and the first electric railway. This freedom from tradition and identity straitjackets may also explain how a band from Düsseldorf managed to become a source of ideas for Black musicians in Detroit or Chicago.

If you listen to the records of Amon Düül, Agitation Free, Ash Ra Tempel, Can, Kluster, Embryo, Guru Guru, Faust, Neu!, Kraftwerk, Popol Vuh, Conrad Schnitzler, Klaus Schulze or Tangerine Dream, you will be at a loss to find the answer to the question of what was musically common to krautrock, and what characterised its style. It becomes even more confusing when you add the names of other German bands from the same period to the list, such as Birth Control, Jane, Bröselmaschine or Ton Steine Scherben. The spectrum ranges from stoned, endless blues rock to cold electric sounds, from metallic noise collages to sugar-sweet, eclectic ethno-sounds, from rock and roll to minimalist organ clusters. Where is the common ground? The spectrum ranges from Kraftwerk's optimistic affirmation of modernity to Popol Vuh's avowed anti-modernism. The contradiction is also expressed visually in Kraftwerk's borrowings from Soviet art of the 1920s on the one hand, and Popol Vuh's romantic mishmash of religious symbolism and wanderlust on the other. Between these two extreme positions there are not only many intermediate stations, but also music that defies the usual krautrock labelling, such as Anima, inspired by Viennese Actionism, or the bands of jazz pianist Wolfgang Dauner. The most common answer to the question of the common musical denominator is: something with electronics. Krautrock is often praised for introducing the synthesiser into pop music. But even among the bands whose sound was essentially characterised by the use of electronic instruments, the range is so wide that simply describing the technical means used, is not enough to form a coherent genre.

If you search for Kraftwerk on Wikipedia, you will find

them categorised as electropop – and if you read on, it says: "Kraftwerk influenced numerous musical styles such as synth-pop, electro-funk, Detroit techno ..." Synth pop is a perfectly appropriate term if you understand it less as the use of synthesisers, and more as the synthetic nature of the music and the image created by the band. It was the synthetic and the cosmopolitan that freed the sound from traditions or any folklore tied to a particular nation. What began as a locational disadvantage for German bands, who found it difficult to write songs like English or American bands, that could draw on the wealth of folk, blues, musicals or music hall, had developed into an advantage. They had to completely reinvent themselves, although they were not entirely without role models. The sound concepts and musical strategies that could be heard on Kluster's records from the early 1970s, or on the first Tangerine Dream LP, had their forerunners in the music of English groups such as AMM or the first Pink Floyd albums. Kraftwerk did not invent synth pop. The fact that it can be attributed to British authors is somewhat surprising, as it was the staff of the BBC's Radiophonic Workshop who produced one of the first electro pop singles in 1962: "Waltz in Orbit" by Ray Cathode. The composers behind this pseudonym were George Martin (later the Beatles producer) and Maddalena Fagandini. One of the first synth pop LPs also came from England: *An Electric Storm* (1969) by White Noise. The LP was on almost every hippie's record shelf in Germany at the time, and Radiophonic Workshop employees were also significantly involved in its production; among those present were Delia Derbyshire and Brian Hodgson. In the USA, the duo Silver Apples hit the charts in 1968 with an album recorded with drums and frequency generators.

THE MOTORIK BEAT

Another characteristic of krautrock is often referred to as the "motorik beat", which was mainly pioneered by the drummers Jaki Liebezeit (Can) and Klaus Dinger (Kraftwerk, Neu!). Plenty of other groups in the krautrock canon managed without this rhythm, but it is not so machine-like. Anyone who tries to play along with "Yoo Doo Right" from Can's album *Monster Movie* as a drummer, quickly realises this claim that Liebezeit's playing anticipated the stoic beats of rhythm machines is not entirely true, at the very least for the early Can records. The term "motorik" is most fitting for Klaus Dinger, the drummer of Neu!. While Liebezeit, for all the consistency with which he maintained a groove, always responded to changes in the musical context and reacted playfully to them with a bouncy, jazz-inspired timing, Dinger was the prototype of the machine drummer who could not be thrown off by anything. However, reducing the debut album *Neu!* to the first track of the LP ("Hallogallo") does it an injustice. The album also contains long passages that manage without a continuous rhythm. But, whenever *Neu!* is spoken or written about, whenever a piece supposedly typical of the band is to be played, it is promptly "Hallogallo". There was hardly any communication with the instruments; the rest of the music had to subordinate itself to the beat. The "motorik beat" is also not suitable as a defining characteristic of krautrock because the opposite also existed: the complete dissolution of linear, repetitive time structures in the music of Kluster or Tangerine Dream. Tangerine Dream's 1972 album *Zeit* consists of music pulsating in slow motion, where sounds develop over long periods of time without any recognisable destination. Even Can, who are often seen as the prototype of primarily rhythmic music, released long, free sound collages on their records that work without a continuous beat.

For this, Stockhausen coined the term 'Klangzeit'. He formulated his idea of a new music in 1963 in the aforementioned concert in the series *Music in the Technical Age* as follows: "Two main criteria: equal status for the participating musicians, meaning that everyone has a turn and tells the others what happens next through what they do. And what happens next depends on the music itself and not on an abstract time that is superimposed on the music. It can be felt very clearly when they (the musicians) watch out for each other like spitz dogs and listen to what the other has just played – and then add their sound and thus there is a constant exchange between the musicians." However, only a few were brave enough to depart from what is called abstract time here and where the ticking of the metronome is meant. Kluster and the first record by Tangerine Dream – both with the collaboration of Conrad Schnitzler – are examples of this. Stockhausen's theory also applies to the first two LPs by Cluster – their name changing after Schnitzler's departure, being spelled with a "C" instead of the original "K". Their music also fulfils another demand of the post-war avant-garde: the equal status of noise and (musical) sound. A video of Tangerine Dream surfaced some time ago showing the band in the Electronik Beat Workshop run by Swiss composer Thomas Kessler – the recording studio set up in a West Berlin school for the then-flourishing amateur band scene. In the same year that they can be seen in a concert filmed by the West Berlin TV station SFB as a trio inspired by Cream, they also play as a trio in the Beat Workshop, albeit with a different line-up. Steve Joliffe (Steamhammer) plays flute, Fred Braceful plays drums, with Edgar Froese as the only "real" Tangerine Dream member on guitar. Above all, the free playing of Fred Braceful, who later played with Wolfgang Dauner and then Exmagma, created a sound that nobody would associate with Tangerine Dream. Here, what you hear is even more consistently oriented towards the idea of Klangzeit than the first LP *Electronic Meditation*.

Perhaps it also mattered which age cohort you belonged to. Schnitzler, Roedelius from Kluster, Holger Czukay and Irmin Schmidt from Can were born before the war. Jaki Liebezeit was born in 1938 and thus belonged to the generation for whom jazz was the soundtrack to a longing for a better outside world – for otherness. These musicians still perceived the swinging timing of jazz as a liberation from marching music and the steady beat of the bass drum. For the musicians who were socialised via beat and rock, a continuous rhythm that structured the music was a matter of course. However, there is still a long way to go between the elastic, body-flattering groove of soul and the rigid beat of techno. But how one deals with musical time is more than just a question of taste. It is also about the temporal organisation of social interaction: from the coordination of rowers, which was already ensured by a drummer in ancient Egypt, to the most pleasant form – dance (which can certainly be subversive as well) – particularly when it resists against a ruling time regime, such as swing did during the Third Reich, or rock and roll in post-war Germany. Capitalism detaches the measurement of time from concrete social action, so that it becomes the linear time of the chronometer, and thus the measure of the determination of labour and value. In *Modern Times*, Charlie Chaplin visualised the contradiction between living and chronometric time when, as an assembly line worker, he unintentionally sabotages the production process because he is unable to adapt to the work cycle of the conveyor belt. At the end of the scene, he shows how subjugation to mechanical time changes even the most human of things. When he encounters a woman in front of the factory gate, he approaches her with the mechanical movements and spanners of the work he has just escaped.

The resistance of the Swingjugend during the Nazi regime was already directed against the rule of chronometric time. In Austria, the young people who preferred the elastic physicality of swing to the goose step called themselves Schlurfs (shufflers). They preferred shuffling to marching. The question of how to deal with time was also discussed in the musical avant-garde. György Ligeti composed his *Poème Symphonique* for 100 metronomes in 1962. Although they all have the same beat, each metronome has its own tempo, which creates the most complex rhythmic overlaps. Until, one by one, each metronome stops when the spring runs out – each in its own time. In these debates, chronometric time was regarded as something not inherent to music, as something externally determined – as a constraint that allowed no alternative. Instead, the temporal sequence and duration of sounds should be something that developed out of musical interaction. This is where the avant-garde of serious music met the ideas of free jazz musicians. Groups such as Just Music, founded at the end of the 1960s by Frankfurt saxophonist Alfred Harth, emerged. Just Music described their concept as "domination-free music". This referred to the lack of division of labour between soloist and accompanists, to the communicative negotiation of the collective process, and also to the free use of time, which depended solely on the current musical occurrences and the spontaneous decisions of the musicians.

An important step in the development of improvised music (actually, parallel to the capitalised "N" in New Music, one should write: Improvised Music) was the departure of percussionists from the role of mere timekeepers. Parallel to the suspension of tonality, linear time dissolved, with new music being the source of ideas here, as well as the preoccupation with non-European (above all, Asian) musical traditions, with the mediation of John Cage playing an important role. Derek Bailey spoke of the musical moment, the now, as the "now now". But this now is not isolated. It contains the future as a possibility, and at the same time the shadow of the past. And every new now is a different now, in which the past nows have been deposited as layers with different after-effects. Improv musicians, such as Tony Oxley, thus arrived at a concept of time that had been discussed in new music for some time.

In this way, musicians approached Theodor W. Adorno's jazz critique, probably without knowing it. Although it must be said with a qualification: Adorno's criticism of the jazz that he likely knew. Before his exile, it was probably the records available in Europe and their adaptation by European dance musicians. The result is well known: Adorno rejected jazz outright. What he wrote about it nevertheless contains a few interesting thoughts. For him, jazz was a product formatted by the culture industry, which only feigned freedom by playing around the established rules of conventional music, not by truly abolishing them. He makes this clear, for example, in the playing of the soloists, whose supposed freedom is limited by the continuous harmony and time sequence of the chorus. In his *Musical Aphorisms* there is a passage in which Adorno speculates about a jazz whose metrics and harmonies dispense with symmetry and cadences, thus overcoming the boundary to art music. The free atonality and liberation from the constraints of an inescapably structured time, as can be heard in the most radical moments of both krautrock and improvised music, comes quite close to this demand. Felix

Klopotek writes in *How They Do It – Free Jazz, Improvisation & Niemandsmusik* about the leap from the limited freedom of the soloist in jazz until bebop's arrival, and the next consequential step toward free jazz as a phase that "left behind the classical song and blues schemes as the basis for improvisation. No longer bound to fixed harmonic-melodic material and rhythmically dissolving the 4/4 time into a multidirectional pulsation, the free jazzers gained their own access to noise as an integrated part of playing. Its production was conceived and practised decidedly as a group process – music-making as a social act was already realised here."

Klopotek's free jazz writings also apply to some krautrock bands upon their departure away from their rock heritage. The musicians who came from rock also became increasingly dissatisfied with their role as service providers for the entertainment industry, which forced them to play largely formatted and functional music. In order to break out of this trap, the krautrockers also began to free themselves from rigid concepts of time and, without much theoretical ballast, looked for ways out of the predetermined patterns. Even if this rarely happened as radically as it did in free jazz, the musicians refused to conform to the expectations of record companies and audiences. The television recording of a Kraftwerk concert from 1970 shows the resulting conflict: Ralf Hütter begins with a Sun Ra-inspired improvisation on an electronic keyboard that lasts several minutes. The audience reacts in a sceptical manner, or even dismissively, and only warm up when a stoic beat eventually kicks in.

Most of the musicians took "do your own thing" seriously. So seriously, in fact, that after their initial interest, most record companies removed krautrock from their catalogues when they realised that the bands were unable or unwilling to adapt to any trends. They were too unpredictable for commercial exploitation. Calculability, however, is only an artistic criterion to a limited extent. It is primarily an economic term. It is about a product that can be reproduced at a predictable cost, where the customer knows what they are getting for their money. The appealing thing about early krautrock was that it largely rejected such economic thinking, and often consciously saw itself as the antithesis of it. The circle of musicians who relate positively to krautrock today is probably just as heterogeneous as krautrock was 50 years ago. For many, however, it is probably precisely this striving for autonomy that makes krautrock interesting for them.

JAZZ

If you look at the biographies of the musicians in the later krautrock bands, you can roughly distinguish between two age groups with different musical socialisations. For those born during the war or directly after it, jazz was the music that embodied the longing for the outside world. Irmin Schmidt from Can was born in 1937, Holger Czukay in 1938, Mani Neumeier, the drummer from Guru Guru in 1940, and bassist Uli Trepte in 1941 – they all started out in jazz bands. Jazz didn't only become a musical vehicle of progressiveness and opposition after the Second World War. This development had already begun after the First World War. When the USA entered the war in 1917, large numbers of American soldiers arrived in Europe – and with them, jazz. The gramophone ensured the further spread of this exciting new music. In what was probably the first book published in Germany about jazz, *Jazz und Shimmy – Brevier der neuesten Tänze* (published by

F. W. Koebner in 1921), the following passage by Hans Siemsen can be found: "And jazz has another nice quality – it is so completely undignified. It smashes any semblance of dignity, of correct posture, of poise, of a stand-up collar – into the ground. Those afraid of making fools of themselves can't dance to it. The German head teacher cannot dance to it. The Prussian reserve officer cannot dance to it. If only all ministers and privy councillors and professors and politicians were obliged to dance to jazz in public from time to time. What a cheerful way they would be stripped of all their dignity! How human, how nice, how funny they would become! No haze of stupidity, vanity and dignity could form. If the Kaiser had danced to jazz – none of all this would ever have happened! But alas, he could never have learnt how. It's easier to be the German Kaiser than to dance to jazz."

"All this" was the First World War. A second one was to follow. In the intervening years, jazz was a liberation from the strict discipline and physical regulation, of both the Prussian barracks and the labour routine of the factories. This came to an end in 1933. The National Socialists' hatred of jazz and new music culminated in the poster for the *Degenerate Music* exhibition, which showed a caricature of a Black man with bulging lips and frizzy hair blowing a saxophone and wearing a Jewish star on his lapel. National Socialism didn't just have the support of its registered party members; the culturally chauvinistic bourgeoisie and its idea of high culture also did to a large extent – especially the music industry personnel in the orchestras and conservatories. After 1945, these personnel were still there, entrenching themselves behind a supposedly completely apolitical, pure art.

For young people from mostly middle class backgrounds who were orientated towards the West (where people could

Previous side: Embryo, 1972. This side: Cluster

Events in the Zodiak, West Berlin

Can, Musikhalle Hamburg, 1972

This side: Kluster
Right side above: Cluster, 1971
Bottom right side: Brian Eno with Cluster

This side: Guru Guru
Right side above: Rio Reiser (Ton Steine Scherben)
Bottom right side: Ton Steine Scherben, 1973

This side: Arnulf Meifert (Faust), 1971
Left side above: Faust, 1971
Bottom right side: Zappi (Faust, 1971)

GURU GURU LIVE

Bernd Sehab

Ax Genrich

Mani Neumeier

Left side above: Anima-Sound
Bottom left side: Neu!
This side: Guru Guru poster, 1973

Faust, 1971

afford records and record players), jazz became all the more of a musical escape from the nationalistic delusion. Anyone who was not in the mood for lockstep and drill and, above all, the rigid gender order of National Socialism, could escape enforced conformity for a few hours at swing dances. Initially, the repressive apparatus, which was not put off by proletarian insubordination, reacted somewhat hesitantly. But then the persecution of the Swingjugend began. There was a similar movement in France with the Zazous. But while the US army was welcomed as a liberator in France and jazz provided the soundtrack, the music still had a hard time in Germany unless it was presented in the conventional delivery offered by the big dance orchestras. For large sections of the bourgeoisie clinging to their supposed cultural superiority, it was the music of the occupying forces.

The jazz that was played in pubs in the early 1960s was mostly dixieland, or a mix of hits and jazz standards played in the swing idiom. Although this provided the musicians with a reasonably secure livelihood, it was not an environment in which musical innovation could flourish. This changed when, at the beginning of the 1960s, these venues gradually began to hire DJs or play music from a tape recorder, as suitable playback technology was invented and available. The musicians suddenly found themselves without their usual audience. Economically, this was a big problem, but artistically it gave them the opportunity to reorient themselves. The main role model here was cool jazz, or the attempts to synthesise jazz and serious music, summarised under the label "third stream". For German musicians with an almost exclusively classical education, these were the most accessible styles in jazz and offered the opportunity to emphasise their soloistic skills, while remaining true to a traditional understanding of craftsmanship.

A good number of the musicians who would later play in krautrock bands began their careers in jazz formations. This applies to Hütter and Schneider (Kraftwerk), but also Jaki Liebezeit (Can), Lothar Meid (Amon Düül), Christian Burchard (Embryo), Arnulf Meifert (Faust), Uli Trepte and Mani Neumaier (Guru Guru) – all musicians who were old enough at the end of the 1960s to look back on a musical biography. The switch to rock music was not difficult for them, because jazz was not perceived as outdated in Germany at the end of the 1960s. As early as 1958, the magazine *Schlagzeug* lamented the "corset of conventionality" in which German jazz musicians would perform the results of their "handicraft lessons" in "dust-free tailored clothing". In the same article, however, the author is pleased that the "striped socks era" has passed, and that jazz is no longer an "amusement hour for dodgy characters". The senior teachers had successfully overcome the initial enthusiasm of jazz in the post-war years, as well as the subversive hedonism of the Swingjugend, scaring off everyone for whom jazz was supposed to be fun.

Those born from around 1948 onwards were followed by a generation whose first attempts at music had taken place in beat bands, and whose role models were no longer Thelonious Monk or John Coltrane, but Chuck Berry and The Rolling Stones: Michael Rother, born in 1950 (Neu!), Manuel Göttsching, born in 1952 (Ash Ra Tempel), Lutz Ulbrich, born in 1952 (Agitation Free). Rock and beat music, which was mainly played by amateurs in Germany at the beginning, took on an unbridled enthusiasm for experimentation from the mid-1960s onwards. It was played by the children of the middle class, which had grown and gained influence in the years of the post-war boom, and a working class that no longer had to struggle in order to secure its material existence.

Guitarists soon realised that the electrical circuit consisting of a player, strings, pickup, amplifier and loudspeaker was a completely new instrument, whose sonic possibilities enabled them to connect with contemporary electronic and electro-acoustic music. Until then, this sort of music had led a rather esoteric existence in prohibitively expensive studios, usually financed by broadcasters or state institutions. This development opened up a new world of sound and unimagined expressive possibilities for guitarists, allowing them to dethrone the previous king of expressivity, the saxophone. The louder you turned it up, the better. Jimi Hendrix's amplifier towers not only produced volume, but also an interaction between musician and sound that could not be achieved without them. There was also the psychological effect: this technology gave players a previously unknown power with which to assert themselves. The old world was made unmistakably clear: nobody listens to you any more, now it's our turn.

FREE JAZZ

With free jazz, a type of music came onto the scene that left behind both the dance music legacy and the endeavours of bourgeois respectability. One of the protagonists of this new music was someone who had an artistic education, though not a musical one: the graphic artist Peter Brötzmann. The connection between jazz and modern painting had existed since the 1920s. Painters from George Grosz to Piet Mondrian to Jackson Pollock were inspired by jazz. This connection also worked in the opposite direction. In Peter Niklas Wilson's book *Hear and Now – Thoughts on Improvised Music*, there is a quote from Keith Rowe, the guitarist of the British group AMM: "If you had studied Marcel Duchamp and Picasso, later the American abstract expressionists, the ideas developed by Robert Rauschenberg, the concepts of John Cage, then the chorus routine in jazz seemed so static and boring that we wanted to develop our own answers."

It was the gesture in Jackson Pollock's drip paintings, for example, and the fascination with the white canvas, which is not a blank space in these paintings but an equal part of the composition, that inspired the musicians to develop a pointillist style. And pictures were no longer "pictures of something" – they were simply pictures, paintings. This coincided with the self-image of the musicians, for whom their music was no longer thematically bound, utility music or illustration, but the exploration of sound.

"Free Jazz – Pop Jazz – incomprehensible or popular?" – this was the title of a 1967 television discussion between the Klaus Doldinger Quartet and the Peter Brötzmann Trio, hosted by Siegfried Schmidt-Joos. The studio set-up was reminiscent of a tribunal, with half a dozen jazz experts from the feature pages of the most important newspapers shrouded in thick cigarette smoke in the role of judges, before whom the two groups had to perform. The youngest member of the panel, Manfred Miller from Radio Bremen and a Jazz Podium author, was the only one to speak in favour of free jazz. While the other experts still carefully weighed up the pros and cons and did not reject free jazz outright, Klaus Doldinger advocated for the proper craft and a guild code that first demanded the proven acquisition of traditional qualifications, before anyone may dare to play something new. He leveled the classic accusations at Peter Brötzmann, which had apparently gone unnoticed by Doldinger when they were applied to the fields of sculpture and painting years before. Brötzmann had not practised at all and should have played something "proper" first. Brötzmann's reply that he didn't think it was necessary to practise something he didn't want to play really infuriated Doldinger. When Brötzmann then replied to the question as to which system he was playing in – "I am the system" – any chance of agreement was finally eliminated.

When Peter Brötzmann was due to play at the West *Berlin Jazztage* in 1968, he was asked to sign a contract stipulating that the musicians had to dress properly. Brötzmann disregarded this and, together with other free jazz musicians, founded the *Total Music Meeting* as a counter-event, which was to remain an important forum for free music for three decades. Free jazz had opened a new door. The krautrockers adopted the improvisational concept and the search for new sounds, but realised this with the means of rock music, which at the time was still exciting, new and experimental. The self-organisation of the free jazzers also became a model for the krautrock scene. One of the first records self-produced by a band was the LP *Machine Gun* by the Peter Brötzmann Trio. In 1969, Brötzmann was one of the founders of Free Music Production (FMP), the first and longest-running German indie label. Brötzmann was accepted by the krautrockers because of his radicalism – though not necessarily listened to. He was too berserk for the mellow stoners. Even the "Frei sein, high sein, Terror muss dabei sein" bands that played at the West Berlin teach-ins of the "Rambling Hash Rebels" were too tender and bourgeois for that. Some jazz musicians tried to jump on the krautrock bandwagon. Even Klaus Doldinger, who had only upheld solid craftsmanship and clean-cut appearance and music, tried it with the formation Doldinger's Motherhood. Wolfgang Dauner, an established jazz pianist, made several attempts with his bands Et Cetera and The Oimels. It was all technically sound, but lacked the right image. Musically most interesting was the LP *Output*, which he recorded together with drummer Fred Braceful, whose free playing had already helped Tangerine Dream to one of their more intriguing moments a few years earlier – in a session from which unfortunately only a few minutes are documented in a West Berlin SFB broadcast. Dauner's handling of the synthesiser is particularly interesting, showing that more is possible with it than just producing endlessly long tones with a heavy hand resting on the keyboard.

TOTALLY FREE MUSIC

John Cage exerted an even greater influence than Karlheinz Stockhausen, whose insistence on the role of the composer was too restrictive for musicians who rebelled against a repressive society. Cage had postulated early on that any sound could be utilised musically – both consciously-produced sounds and environmental noises. For him, silence was also a means of musical expression. Above all, however, instead of a fixed composition, he introduced an open form and chance.

John Cage's musical ideas, such as playing random records or listening to radio stations in concert, only had a limited effect in an academic context, yet they questioned the role of the composer. The Fluxus movement became a transmission belt. As action art, Fluxus was always more than just a branch of the visual arts. The overlap with music was great from the very beginning and is expressed in the biographies of a number of Fluxus artists who were active in both fields. John Cage's class for experimental composition at the New

School for Social Research in New York was also attended by "non-musicians" – including a number of later Fluxus artists such as Al Hansen, Yoko Ono and George Maciunas. What they had in common was a rejection of the "great" work for the art market, and an emphasis on the social and processual nature of their work in "flux". Fluxus concerts are small, collage-like scores that record a series of choreographic, visual, textual and musical actions, the execution of which leaves plenty of room for interpretation and chance. The proximity to the working method of improvised music is unmistakable. And so is the shared love of the ephemeral, which is inherent in music anyway.

A scratched, faded piece of cine film from 1962 shows the then 23-year-old Peter Brötzmann on stage. Free jazz? Not a saxophone to be seen. Brötzmann is a participant at a Fluxus festival in Wiesbaden initiated by George Maciunas. The event was billed as a *Fluxus Internationale Festspiele Neuester Music* (Fluxus International Festival of Newest Music), but there was no distinction between happening, performance and music. Newest Music was deliberately chosen as the title to distinguish it from the new music that began with Arnold Schönberg, which was no longer so new at the time. Above all, for all its musical radicalism, new music was still rooted in the old structures: the composer as genius creator, the musicians as performing organs and the audience as passive consumers. In the 1960s, Intermedia and Fluxus became the motto and designation of an art that ignored the old genre boundaries. Visual artists such as Joseph Beuys and Wolf Vostell used sound as a means in their art actions. When art production was taken out of the seclusion of the studio and made public, the resulting sounds also became part of the actions, such as when Vostell smashed light bulbs on a plexiglass wall erected between him and the audience. In another action, Vostell blurred photos from magazines with the help of a solvent, amplifying the resulting scraping and scratching noises with a microphone. In this way, Vostell turned the production of images into music. Visual art thus took on the eventful and processual nature of music, and lost its claim to eternity.

For Vostell, the excursion into noise music remained an episode. Ben Patterson, a successful classical double bass player, switched completely to visual art under the influence of the Fluxus happenings. Conrad Schnitzler went the other way round, taking his sculptures to a forest clearing, where they may even still stand today, and devoting himself entirely to music. The announcement of a concert at the *Information Art Festival* in Kiel in 1971 documents how closely he remained connected to the ideas of Fluxus, with a poster showing the entire spectrum of krautrock with photos ranging from Peter Brötzmann to the Scherben. Schnitzler announced the contribution of his group Eruption as follows: "The audience brings small transistor radios, receives an admission discount and is obliged to make music in the hall with the transistor radios. The audience is given violins to play, which send their filtered sounds into the room via the electric amplifiers, coupled with the light action system, which follows the intentions of the players. (Violins are considered a classical instrument and are regarded with reverence by those around them). With the help of the audience, a large canvas is attached to a frame and the audience paints the picture over the course of days." The "desecration" of the violins was in keeping with the destruction of the piano during Fluxus happenings. For the Fluxus artists, the piano was the incarnation of a culture of domination that needed to be dismantled.

Eruption was not the only "artist band". In Düsseldorf, also in Joseph Beuys' circle, Pissoff was formed in 1967 with the painter and sporadic Kraftwerk member Eberhard Kranemann. Peter Brötzmann played together with the Fluxus artists George Brecht and Emmett Williams. One half from which Faust was formed was a group based around the Hamburg art school, which was also more inspired by radical art movements than by rock and roll, which they didn't want to play, or simply couldn't play – whereby they then made a virtue out of this necessity. It is no longer possible to determine how many such groups there were, as they hardly left behind any recordings. It often remained a radical initial phase, which then came to an end when they tried to join the normal music scene. As with Amon Düül, this then led to a split, at the end of which the musicians continued with a professionalised and largely predictable programme. "Real" musicians struggled with the artists' ideas. When Conrad Schnitzler introduced electrically amplified, deliberately non-musical noises to Tangerine Dream, Klaus Schulze, who played drums at the time, complained that Schnitzler "just wanted to ruin everything". Only flyers and a handful of photos exist of the line-up, with which Tangerine Dream played a programme entitled *Our Daily Work* at Frankfurt's TAT – Theater am Turm in 1969. The flyer announces Tangerine Dream as "Germany's freest beat band". The band "reproduces the music production of everyday life. (...) intoning work and pleasure". The band was supported by action artist Bernhard Höke and his self-made noise instruments. The most radical sounds of krautrock came from people who had come to that path via the fine arts, and were completely free from the craftsmanly ethos of jazz and rock musicians.

SPEECHLESS

Lyrics played only a minor role in krautrock. The songs were either instrumental or the vocals were used as a sound, as another instrument. Krautrock did not produce any star singers – no Van Morrison, Mick Jagger or Joe Cocker. The few, mostly English lyrics of the krautrockers were less about making a statement than about creating that otherness that symbolised a world beyond everyday German life in which people felt so ill-at-ease. Frank Apunkt Schneider rightly calls English a "language of longing" in his book *Deutschpop halt's Maul* (German Pop, Shut Your Mouth). The same applies to the sound and the musical material, to the popularity of the bands in particular, in whose sound the African-American heritage of the blues was unmistakable. In terms of sound, it was hardly more possible to distance pop music from Germany. It barely mattered that the lyrics could only be understood in fragments. Nevertheless, this was perceived as a shortcoming and a whole generation, for whom English had previously been just another school subject, developed the ambition to learn the language. They were often better at speaking it than their English teachers, who were overwhelmed by all the colloquialisms and insinuations in the lyrics.

The beat bands of the time were completely satisfied with their epigonal status, with their "secondarity", as Schneider calls it. This was not perceived as an inability, but as a ticket to participate in a transnational cultural movement that liberated them from Germany. What was important to them was not showing off their own creativity, but rather a non-identity, a cheerful proclamation of not belonging. Frank Apunkt Schneider calls this the "next escalation stage of self-alienation", an escape from the existing identity by young Germans through copying the attitude to life of young Brits – who in turn looked across the Atlantic.

Musically, this still worked to some extent, even if there was a lack of traditions to draw on. From folk and blues to British music hall, there was nothing comparable to be found in Germany. But the most difficult thing were the lyrics. What role models, especially in contemporary literature, could we have as references? Until the mid-1960s, there was no equivalent to Allen Ginsberg, Jack Kerouac or William S. Burroughs in Germany. The literary pool and personal relationships to writers from which a John Lennon, a Lou Reed or a Bob Dylan drew were missing in Germany. German contemporary literature in those years was called Group 47, and even that was quite old. Above all, the authors of Group 47 endeavoured to reproduce the elitist concept of high culture.

Even more problematic, however, was the way in which Group 47 dealt with the German past, encouraging an interpretation of history that stylised the Germans as victims. Early on, texts written by members of Group 47 equivalised the suffering in concentration camps, the Allied air war and the expulsion from the eastern formerly German territories. Emigrants were not necessarily welcome in Group 47, an experience that many returnees had faced – not only authors. When Marlene Dietrich returned to West Germany for the first time for a tour in 1960, she was insulted and spat at as a traitor to the fatherland. The slogan "Never again Germany" is said to have originated here as Dietrich's comment on these events. When Paul Celan read his "Death Fugue" at a Group 47 conference in 1952 – "death is a master from Deutschland" – it caused a scandal. Conference participants made fun of Celan's treatment of the Holocaust and Hans Werner Richter, the initiator of the group, commented on Celan's lecture as "singsong read out like in a synagogue".

The language of Group 47 was not only non-sensuous, it was also unmusical. There was nothing to be gained from transforming it into song lyrics, and younger people didn't like to hear the self-stylisation as a victim either. It was familiar from terrible evenings at family celebrations, when the cognac was on the table after a big meal and the men in the family started talking about the war. Group 47's star began to sink in the second half of the 1960s, when a new generation of authors appeared on the scene, such as Peter Handke. His appearance at a Group 47 conference in the USA turned into a scandal, as Handke, instead of angling for the career-promoting effects of such a network, dared to openly confront it and declared the group's programme to be "ludicrous descriptive literature" and the gestures of this language to be "completely dull". Erich Kuby wrote about this appearance in 1966 in *Der Spiegel* magazine, in language that shows how this group of men, who felt steeled by their war experience, thought about Handke: "This girly-boy Peter with his hair combed daintily over his ears, with his little blue peaked cap, one is almost tempted to say: with his little blue peaked cap, his tight knickers, his gentle Easter egg face ..."

Handke was the first of a new generation of authors who stood for a new attitude to life that was essentially characterised by beat music. The stage directions for *Offending the Audience*, his 1966 attack on the passively consuming, educated middle-class theatre audience, stated that the actors should draw inspiration from beat music. The play ran for a long time at the Forum Theatre, West Berlin's most experimental theatre.

Photos of Handke wearing a moptop, leaning casually against the amplifiers of a beat band and the announcement

"Beat & Lyrik" could be seen in the showcases. Also in 1966, Hubert Fichte read from his novel *The Palette*, accompanied by a beat band, to a full house at the Starclub in Hamburg, where the Beatles had started out a few years earlier. Something comparable to American Beat literature had emerged, which quite openly questioned the old division between high culture, and the supposedly inferior and commercial pop culture. Rolf Dieter Brinkmann wrote about this new sensuality in *Acid*: "In 1964, 100 million Elvis Presley records had already been sold. This means that it is a movement that is no longer primarily determined by literarisation, yet by no means excludes the literary. Mixtures are taking place – images interspersed with words, sentences rearranged into images and visual (imaginary) contexts, record albums presented like books."

If you listen to Fichte's reading today, you realise that literature and music remain separate, in contrast to British or American models. Fichte reads a passage from his story about the Hamburg subculture of non-conformists, bums, gays, artists and stoners, then the band plays. The songs were the standard repertoire that almost every band of those years played, with English lyrics – there was no need for German lyrics. Even though there were new authors who were beat fans and probably wanted nothing more than to follow in Bob Dylan's footsteps, the convergence of music and literature did not work in Germany. Not even when the authors were connected to the relevant scene. In *Acid*, Brinkmann wrote the blueprint for the connection between literature and psychedelic music: "Familiar literary patterns of imagination become blurred: space expands, altered dimensions of consciousness. The feedback system of words, which functions in familiar grammatical orders, no longer corresponds to everyday sensory experience." Can came very close to this concept. Nowhere more so than in Jerzy Skolimowski's 1970s film *Deep End*, in which Can's music provides the soundtrack for a chase through Soho, which at the time was still a red-light district, an amusement district and the centre of pop music. The fact that krautrock favoured open forms over the self-contained song format, made this music ideal for combining with visual media. Film music became an important economic pillar of krautrock.

BEAT-CLUB, RE-EDUCATION AND SEXPOL

In the early 1960s, small, cheap transistor radios came onto the market. Portable record players with built-in loudspeakers that could be hidden away in the children's room or taken to a party were popular. If you had a bit more pocket money or already had a job, you bought a tape recorder with which you could record your friends' records. Specialised record shops only existed in the big cities in the 1960s. Otherwise, records were available in a corner of the local electronics shop, where the range was limited to classical music, German "Schlager" pop hits and what is known as Volksmusik – not real folk music, but rather a kind of commercialised Germanic folksiness that is mostly kitsch. Rock and roll and beat were in short supply, except for the best-known groups from the hit parade. Record companies still gave the shopkeepers leaflets on which they instructed the sales staff on the phonetic pronunciation of the English titles: "Konni Frahnziss" for Connie Francis or "Rannewäi" for Del Shannon's hit "Runaway". Food for the tape recorder also came from the Allied broadcasters, AFN and BFBS. Anyone who lived in their broadcasting area was fortunate. You were even better off if you could also listen to Radio Luxembourg, or even one of the pirate stations broadcasting from ships off the English and Dutch coasts.

Not everyone had the opportunity to listen to their favourite music live either. "Live" usually meant local bands in some dance hall or pub. You had to be of the right age and have the right amount of money. You were best off if you lived in a big city like Munich or Hamburg, or in a town like Hanau with its large US garrison, around which an infrastructure catering to the tastes of the GIs had developed. German radio programmes, on the other hand, were a desert until the end of the 1960s. From September 1965, people waited all the more for the *Beat-Club* produced by Radio Bremen for German television.

In the beginning, bands performed live there, well-known and less well-known names, even musicians at the beginning of their careers. The bands played on a flat stage, barely visible over the heads of the dancing audience. The audience was anything but a passive consumer, but rather an active participant whose appropriation of the pop-cultural goods was a creative construction of their own identity. In the *Beat-Club* studio, the image of a lively youth culture was to be created. This could only work to a very limited extent under the spotlights and cameras. But as awkward as the result may seem today, its impact back then was huge. The idea came from Ernest Bornemann, born in 1915, the son of Jewish parents who managed to flee to England in 1933 with forged papers as an exchange student. In Berlin, he had worked in a German Communist Party counselling centre that advised young workers on sexual issues and distributed contraceptives.

These advice centres were part of the organisation German Reich Association for Proletarian Sexual Politics, abbreviated to Sexpol, co-founded by Wilhelm Reich. Reich, who combined psychoanalysis and Marxist theory, soon came into conflict with the communist party, as he criticised its authoritarian policies, which were aligned with the Soviet Union under Stalin. In particular, his book *The Mass Psychology of Fascism*, in which Reich opposed the purely economic explanation for the success of fascism, led to conflicts that ended in his expulsion from the party. Reich argued that unemployment and social misery alone could not explain the appeal of fascist ideology. The National Socialists had also been successful among relatively secure skilled workers, employees and large sections of the middle classes. Reich referred to the authoritarian character created by upbringing in the patriarchal family, and the suppression of instincts and disciplining of the body. His political strategy was aimed at prophylaxis through anti-authoritarian education and liberated sexuality.

Reich's writings, which were forgotten after the war, circulated in large print runs from the mid-1960s and were also read by people who were bored by the Marxist classics. With his criticism of authoritarianism, he struck a chord with young people in particular, who suffered most from repressive upbringings and sexual morals. Reich's popularity was not affected by his later descent into esotericism and obscurantism. His theories were not only an explanation for the rise of National Socialism, they also helped to understand why parts of the working class in the German Communist Party defected to the National Socialists. They also revealed the mechanisms by which right-wing ideologies were able to continue in the Federal Republic after the war. Not only in West Germany – Reich also provided a model to explain why the GDR, despite the expropriation of factories and a superficially socialist system, was able to become the unbearable authoritarian state that confronted us: in the form of the People's Police, every time we travelled there from West Berlin. But Wilhelm Reich was not only rediscovered as a theorist. Studying his writings had very practical consequences: the idea of abolishing the nuclear family as a source of authoritarian education, and the Kinderladen movement. The extent of his influence on the German music scene at this time can be seen in statements by bands such as Amon Düül. The idea of the music commune, in which many of the krautrock bands lived for a time, was fuelled by these debates to a large extent.

When Ernest Bornemann returned to Germany from exile, the rediscovery of Wilhelm Reich was still unthinkable. In England and later in Canada, Bornemann had earned his living as a crime novelist. He became more interested in jazz, which he had already loved in Berlin, writing about jazz and blues in Melody Maker and combining this with his ethnological studies. In Germany, he became known as an anthropologist and sex researcher (including "Patriarchy – the origin and future of our social system" and "Sexual market economy – on commodity and sexual intercourse in bourgeois society"). And he was one of the many lateral entrants in radio and television during the 1950s and 1960s – some of whom had returned from exile and, like Bornemann, had already worked for the BBC during the war. As part of the denazification process, the British occupying power paid particular attention to the development of the public broadcasting system.

Cultural policy and the music industry in particular were an important area of re-education from the very beginning. The military government promoted concerts by composers who had been ostracised during the Nazi regime and those who had refused to be instrumentalized for Nazi cultural policy. There wasn't anything like a "black list". Only composers such as Hans Pfitzner, who had openly declared their support for National Socialism, were no longer played (though unfortunately he is again today). The military government also sponsored tours by American musicians. In 1948, Leonard Bernstein conducted concerts in Munich and wrote about his success with German audiences, as Alex Ross quotes him in *The Rest Is Noise*: "It means so much for the American military government, since music is the German's last stand in their 'master-race' claim, and for the first time it's been exploded in Munich." Winifred Wagner, who had directed the *Bayreuth Festival* until 1944 and developed it into a Nazi cult centre, remaining loyal to Hitler until her death in 1980, experienced her own shattering of the master race claim. She felt the greatest humiliation imaginable when Black GIs were billeted in her Bayreuth villa.

The US military government also sponsored events such as the *International Summer Courses for New Music*, where works of the musical avant-garde, pieces by Schönberg, Webern and Bartók, were performed from 1946 onwards. There were also theoretical lectures by lecturers such as Theodor W. Adorno and Heinz-Klaus Metzger. Guests at the holiday courses included Pierre Boulez, Edgard Varèse and John Cage. In his report, however, an employee of the US military administration described his fear that an overly radical break with musical tradition, as demanded at the summer courses, could be counterproductive and offend the music-loving middle class circles that were meant to be won over. Perhaps this is one of the reasons why modern music still has a hard time in the German music scene today. Like jazz, which the military authorities also promoted, and later rock and roll, it was perceived as occupier music – which didn't bother the audience in the *Beat-Club*. They implemented their own cheerful denazification.

Bornemann saw *Beat-Club* in exactly the same way – as a practical contribution to denazification, which he believed was still not complete in 1965. For him, beat music was the right way to reach young people, because he recognised an emancipatory potential in their new approach to the body, the liberation from the corset of rigid posture – even if, as a diehard jazz fan, he only liked the music to a limited extent. Until then, if young people wanted to dance anywhere other than dodgy bars, the only option had been dance school with its strict rules of behaviour, where it made the young men sweat with fear when they had to ask their partner to dance – with a handkerchief so that their hands, wet with fear, didn't leave a stain on a dress. The reactions of the official and self-appointed morality guardians to the *Beat-Club* were correspondingly strong. Bornemann had taken this into account and built it into his concept. In the first *Beat-Club* season, selected letters from viewers were read out – especially those in which the people's outrage was boiling. The effect worked perfectly according to the inventor's plans. The writers of these letters exposed themselves to the audience as the eternally outdated people they really were. These letters and their writers were thus exposed to public dispute and, importantly, public laughter. It can be assumed that the worst letters were not even presented.

Dancing was important to Bornemann, as he saw it as a way of breaking out of rigid physical discipline. Even in the 1920s, with the first enthusiasm for jazz, dancing was a battle zone between reactionaries, who saw the West perishing because of "racial dances", and progressives, who wanted to enjoy freedom after the end of the empire and the horrors of war.

Unfortunately, in the long run Bornemann was unable to prevail against director Michael Leckebusch, who turned the *Beat-Club* into a showcase for the latest products of the record industry. However, this did not go quite as smoothly as he had imagined. When the audience was locked out and the bands only mimed to playback, there were loud protests and from the end of the 1960s the bands played live in the *Beat-Club* again. Music and presentation became more critical as public debates became more politicised. Instead of the three-minute single format, bands could play for longer. There were also short films, critical commentaries and special formats. Bands were presented in detail in so-called workshop concerts, including bloopers and multiple attempts at playing a song. And there were no star fees, just a better expense allowance. The station successfully argued that it was ultimately advertising if the bands could perform on one of the most popular music programmes. All rights remained with the broadcaster, and Radio Bremen still makes a living from it to this day.

INTERMEDIA AND SONG DAYS

At the end of the 1960s, there were several festivals, mostly financed by cities, that wanted to be more than just pure music events, and that became a platform for the developing krautrock scene. *Intermedia 69* was the name of a festival organised by Klaus Staeck and Jochen Goetze in Heidelberg in 1969, which brought together theatre, performance, sculpture, painting, film and music. The event took place in public spaces and student halls of residence. Klaus Staeck washed kitschy oil paintings bought in department stores in the washing machine until only the white canvas remained. Christo wrapped the Amerika-Haus in fabric – a highly controversial action in 1969. The Donata Höffer Band, one of the first West Berlin free jazz bands, and The Guru Guru Groove Band were invited as musical acts. In addition, two groups – Noah's Ark and the Duck Butter Trust – in which visual artists had come together, played non-music in the Fluxus style. All of this still fit into one programme. But almost more important than the actual programme was talking to each other about it – even if that wasn't always easy at the highly politicised end of the 1960s. The poles were the artists' joy of experimentation; the passers-by were often perplexed, and sometimes aggressive, at actions taking place in the urban space, and the part of the left for whom the propaganda kitsch of Chinese posters was the pinnacle of proletarian artistic creation.

At *Intermedia* in Heidelberg, the proportion of music was still relatively small. At other events, it increasingly became the main focus, overshadowing everything else. The *1968 Essen International Song Days*, organised by Rolf-Ulrich Kaiser and financed by the city, were also an attempt to create a mixture of concert, film, theatre and communication. In practice, however, the emphasis shifted in favour of music consumption. At the time, this was still cause for criticism, but over the years the perception has changed to the extent that today the *Song Days* are only remembered as the alleged birth of krautrock – although Frank Zappa's performance with the Mothers of Invention was the musical highlight at the time. The extent to which the narrative of pop music has changed from counterculture to pure event can be seen by watching older documentaries about pop music. There are several films about the *Essen International Song Festival* that illustrate this change. The first film was produced by Bayerischer Rundfunk – the Bavarian state broadcaster – a few weeks after the event.

It deals with the question of the extent to which a music event can fulfil the political claim that the *Song Days* propagated with their image of counterculture, or whether in the end it is merely about consumption. Rolf-Ulrich Kaiser and the festival organisers were very serious about trying to bring music and political debates together. The bands were sent a letter in advance stating: "Songs don't make revolutions; but songs accompany revolutions! Songs will not change society; but they can help!", together with the question: "What contribution do you think songs make to changing society?" The most radical answer was intoned by Franz Josef Degenhardt with his song "Zwischentöne sind nur Krampf im Klassenkampf" (intermediate tones are just a cramp in the class war). On his live album from 1971, Degenhardt summarised his experiences with the counterculture in the song "Die Wallfahrt zum Big Zeppelin" (the pilgrimage to the big zeppelin) – he accused the hippie movement of being "on the wrong trip again with pop and pot, similar to their ancestors, the Wandervögel" – a youth movement from 1896 to 1933. This – and his closeness to the German Communist Party – did not necessarily win Degenhardt many friends. Like most songwriters, he kept his distance from a pop culture that was more interested in the sensual experience than in pedagogically-minded lyrics. The most clear-sighted criticism in the 1968 film came from an unexpected source: Wilhelm Nieswandt, the Lord Mayor of Essen, who had made the 1968 Essen song festival possible in the first place thanks to the city's financial support (which was very generous for those times), put it in a nutshell in an interview: "They just want to sell stuff". And: "You can't change the world with songs. You need dynamite for that!" An unusually clear statement for a social democrat and older gentleman (Nieswandt was already over 70 at the time).

20 years after the *Song Days,* a WDR production was made to mark the anniversary, in which the nostalgically coloured personal memories reveal how important the event once was for the protagonists and participants. The debates about commerce and consumption at the time, in which it was criticised that the 50 hours of music played at the festival were offset by only seven hours of lectures and discussions, now seem merely trivial. Another 20 years later, in the opulent documentary *Kraut & Rüben – über die Anfänge deutscher Rockmusik*, the festival in Essen was stylised as the founding myth of a national pop culture. The originally ironic motto "Germany awake", under which Tangerine Dream and Amon Düül performed in Essen, has lost its ironic subtext. While at the time these musicians were a red rag for conservative Germany, from which the slogan had been stolen, they now serve to create identity and are seen as an economic and export factor. Nevertheless, Edgar Froese, the founder of Tangerine Dream, did not take part in this retrospective glorification. Instead, he soberly stated that after the Mothers of Invention's performance, he understood what league the German bands were playing in.

It was not only television (whose culture departments in the 1960s were staffed by editors who had read their Adorno) that was critical of rock music, which called itself progressive. Conversely, television was also seen by musicians as a means of manipulation. Irmin Schmidt, Can's keyboard player, answered the question about the band's political attitude in an article circa the release of their album *Tago Mago*: "Television is incredibly interested in the political opinions of beat musicians because they can't talk. Television is absolutely not interested in the political opinions of those who also want socialism and a society that is more humane, but who can talk. I am unsure. I know far too little. So I'm supposed to say what I know on television? That little bit? So that television, in its glorious, socially critical function, can take me as an example, and proclaim: 'Look, they don't know what they want'. As I said: I am supposed to take a position in which I am manipulated, and as easily as possible. In other words, I'm supposed to simplify an incredibly complicated economic process so crudely that it becomes consumable. That's an alibi for television. Television realises that the music contains a little – and it can only be a very little – of the revolution we want. But you can destroy that little bit by manipulating the musicians into a situation where they have to interpret their music with words – and that goes 100 percent wrong." 30 years later, Irmin Schmidt would say in a documentary film about Can: "There was never a political message in our music."

UNDERGROUND? POP? NEIN! GEGENKULTUR!

Under this title – *Underground? Pop? Nein! Gegenkultur!* – Rolf-Ulrich Kaiser's book about the flourishing counterculture he had encountered during his visits to the USA was published in 1969. The title referred to a debate from those years. Although underground was a common term, it was also an advertising sticker that CBS stuck on their *That's Underground* records. And were people really underground – under threat of persecution? The majority of alternative culture took place on the open stage. But they didn't want to be pop either. According to the common interpretation in the 1960s, pop stood for commerce. People didn't like subculture either, because the term seemed vague and merely referred to a group within a society that was linked by common characteristics – it could also be allotment gardeners. Counterculture, on the other hand, was a clear statement of not only wanting to be a niche within the dominant culture, but to overcome this dominant culture. In his book, Kaiser listed all sorts of things: from music to street theatre, from filmmakers to the diggers' swap shops in San Francisco. The layout of the volume copied the small and smallest publications of the rapidly growing alternative press. However, this reveals a contradiction that ran through Kaiser's work as an author, producer, concert organiser and label manager. The book was not an underground product, even if it used the stylistic devices of the alternative press in its layout. It was published by a large publishing house, Kiepenheuer & Witsch.

For many, even the term "counterculture" was not radical enough. A flyer from the West Berlin "Central Council of Rambling Hash Rebels" advertising a teach-in at the Technical University in 1969 was emblazoned with the term "super culture" – and the invitation: "Bring shit with you!" A Hash Rebel teach-in could not be organised without music. The band announced was Agitation Free, West Berlin krautrock pioneers. On the comic-style poster, the musicians had enormous joints stuck in their mouths and proclaimed in a speech bubble: "Be high, be free, terror there must be". The slogan "Break what breaks you", later popularised by Ton Steine Scherben, also appeared for the first time on the Hash Rebels' flyers.

An important means of communication in this counterculture was the large number of small underground magazines with circulations ranging from a few thousand to over ten thousand. In addition, there were commercial magazines such as *Sounds*, *Pardon,* or *Konkret* with circulations in the six-figure range, all of which located themselves in the left-wing political coordinate system, and saw themselves as a counter-public and together – unimaginable for left-wing publications today – reaching an audience of millions. The production of underground magazines was enabled by the technological innovation of photochemical offset printing, which made it possible to photograph and reproduce any template. This made these relatively cheap machines the ideal tool for pirate printers. All you needed was a copy of the book you wanted to reprint. Initially, it was not about piracy in the true sense of the word. The first pirated prints were new editions of lost books from the labour movement and left-wing theoretical debates from the time before the National Socialist seizure of power, which remained rare after 1945 because they fell victim to anti-communism in the West and Stalinism in the East. This was particularly true of books that discussed the relationship between Marxism and psychoanalysis. This debate attracted increasing interest as Marxist explanations for the rise of National Socialism, which were reduced to questions of economics, appeared increasingly unsatisfactory.

Offset printing on affordable machines enabled the emergence of a vast number of alternative magazines with names such as Pängg, Hundert Blumen, Charlie Kaputt, Germania or Ulcus Molle, through which the counterculture communicated. Some of these magazines were produced relatively conventionally, with neat typesetting and layout. However, the new technology also made it possible to create a completely different kind of design, abandoning the linear left-to-right typeface and its inherent principle of order. In a collage or cut-up technique, snippets of text, tear-outs from other printed material or images from advertising could be combined with each other however one wanted. Anja Schwanhäußer writes in *Stilrevolte Underground*: "In deliberate friction with and as a counter-strategy to existing texts and images, their natural order was disrupted by cutting them up and rearranging them. The randomly created new combinations were a criticism of the closed social system of meaning, which is expressed in the now cut up material." A further means was the use of material that was regarded by high culture as mass cultural trash, which could be used to attack the high cultural value system. In the beginning, it was the comics of American illustrators such as Robert Crumb or Gilbert Shelton, then later joined by German illustrators.

The underground magazines were the medium in which you could read articles about the hip groups of those years – The Doors, The Rolling Stones, Jimi Hendrix and, time and time again, Frank Zappa and the Mothers Of Invention – as well as texts about the first krautrock bands. Here you could also find out about events where these groups played. This self-portrayal of Tangerine Dream can be found in *Germania*, published in Frankfurt in 1971, which shows how similar the thoughts of the makers of the underground newspapers and the musicians were: "We try to use musical means to reduce the all-too-stable structure of preconceived opinions, habits and pseudo-realities to a neutral point from which some things can perhaps be recognised a little more clearly and free of value categories. (...) Our music does not claim to be definitive. The listener is free to enter at any point of the circle in order to establish a relationship with himself. The experiences we have and the musical realisation we strive for do not only change our own personality. We want to express that there is a human being behind all processes, no matter how complicated. We try to prevent the listener from being forced to react in a certain way by an 'arranged expressiveness'. This is the disastrous basis of most concerts, where it appears that the only thing being offered from the stage is a service in return for the entrance fee. The musician must also offer himself as a commodity."

DRAWING A CLEAR DIVIDING LINE …

At the end of 1971, WDR broadcasted a panel discussion entitled "Pop & Co. – die andere Musik zwischen Protest und Kommerz" (Pop & Co. – the other music between protest and commerce) in the *Ende offen* series, moderated by Hans G Helms, in which all the questions that still haunt the "indie vs. major" debate today were addressed. As the child of a German-Jewish family, Helms had survived the Nazi era with forged papers. After the war, he first went to Sweden, where he played saxophone with Charlie Parker and Gene Krupa. Helms then worked as part of the cultural re-education programme for Allied radio stations, where he was the first to combine poetry and modern jazz. At the *Darmstadt Summer Course*, he served as the translator for John Cage. In his collection of essays *Musik zwischen Geschäft und Unwahrheit* (music between business and untruth), Helms addressed the economic conditions of music production. It was therefore not to be expected that he would uncritically follow the enthusiasm for the counterculture and its musical products.

The late-night programme would have attracted little attention and long been forgotten had it not ended so spectacularly. This ending haunts the world again and again, freed from its original context, as a piece of media history. At the end of the discussion, one of the participants pulled an axe out from under his jacket and, after announcing that he now had to "draw a clear dividing line", attempted to smash the table at which the panel was sitting. An action in the best happening tradition. Back then, people were used to a lot of things, which is why the other panellists didn't feel threatened for a second, but just slid back in their chairs, a little bit irritated. The man with the axe was Nikel Pallat, at the time the manager of the band Ton Steine Scherben, who were one of the first to set up their own label in order to maintain their artistic and political independence.

Rock musicians had a hard time with the idea of producing and distributing their records independently – all their role models were signed to the major labels. The Scherben probably wouldn't have had the idea that they could take record production into their own hands if Klaus Freudigmann, their sound engineer, hadn't had connections to FMP. Free Music Production had been founded in West Berlin before the Scherben and their own label, which they named David Volksmund. The free jazzers around Jost Gebers realised that their music would not reach a large audience, and therefore the commercial record companies would show no interest. After already declaring themselves independent of established jazz festivals and concert operations, the most logical step was to set up a label. For 30 years, the *Total Music Meeting*, organised for the first time in 1968, became an important meeting place for all varieties of free jazz and improvised music.

The free jazz musicians were aware of their marginal position. The 2,000 records sold were a complete success. Rock musicians, on the other hand, orientated themselves on the sales figures of well-known bands. Even three times that amount would have been a flop, and nobody at the record companies would have answered the phone for a band with such meagre sales prospects. FMP also had it easier elsewhere.

The musicians didn't see their records as masterpieces carved in stone, but as documentation of a performance that reflected the current state of their music. A live recording, whose technical complexity and production costs were manageable, was sufficient. Rock musicians, on the other hand, wanted to sound like the big bands from the hit parade. The technical complexity of recording had increased rapidly since the mid-1960s. The Beatles' Sgt Pepper album was still recorded on four tracks, yet a few years later it needed to be at least 16. Experiments could only be afforded to a limited extent with the rising production costs, so simply improvising on the fly became an economic risk.

Half of the Scherben's first album *Warum geht es mir so dreckig?* (Why am I so miserable?) is a live recording of a concert in the canteen at the Technical University of Berlin, which captures the mood and their no-frills sound very well. The other side of the LP consists of recordings in which the band tried to copy the sound of current studio productions without having the necessary technical means or budget. The whole record was originally planned that way. The result created long faces and so the decision was made to record a concert. For the next record, they went into a real studio because they had not given up on the dream of sounding like the greats of rock music. However, the contradiction between the expected sales figures and the production costs, both for the studio and the rapidly growing demands for concert technology, was not only a problem for the Scherben, which left them with a pile of debt in the end. The Scherben showed perseverance and idealism that kept them going into the 1980s. Commercial record companies were more dispassionate in their calculations and, with a few exceptions, after the initial hype they dropped the krautrock bands from their rosters.

But recording and pressing a record is only the first step. Effective distribution is almost more important. One of Rio Reiser's brothers was a pirate printer and in contact with the left-wing bookshops that had sprung up in all major cities, especially university centres, from the mid-1960s onwards. This provided the first distribution network. The band's media presence also helped. It is part of the Scherben legend that the band was on a blacklist, and therefore could not be played on the radio. That may well have been the case during the time of hysteria about the Red Army Faction. In the beginning, however, the band had several television appearances that made them famous. In order to keep production costs low, *Warum geht es mir so dreckig?* had a simple cardboard sleeve, which was stapled together at home by the band. This took away any commodity-like quality, and instead gave it an aura of the underground and a sense of urgency. In addition to bookshops, the Scherben also sold their productions through record shops, which at the time did not yet consist of large chains. Instead, they travelled around the country in a rickety band bus and approached the shops directly. The shops were so surprised by this unusual distribution method that the band managed to sell a few records everywhere. This method was so successful that other bands also started to produce their own records. A network was founded under the name Schneeball (snowball), through which groups such as Embryo, Sparifankerl and Missus Beastly distributed their records together and sold them at concerts. The Scherben thus became the forerunner of the indie labels of the 1980s.

If you look at the course of the WDR television discussion today, in which the Scherben, as representatives of independent production, and Rolf-Ulrich Kaiser, as a representative of the record industry (which he did not consider himself to be), sat opposite each other, you have to realise that the majority of the positions represented were far to the left – a kind of family dispute about who was the most left-wing. Pallat distanced himself from the academic discourse of the other participants by demanding a clear taking of sides and calling music entrepreneurs "capitalist pigs" and "pop gangsters". He labelled groups that are under contract with the industry as "whores". He even gave this title to the band Floh de Cologne, who, like Ton Steine Scherben, combined left-wing positions with German lyrics. After Nikel Pallat had loudly proclaimed that they were making music for the people and not freaky music for specialists, he hit a snag with the counter-question: "And what if the people aren't good?" A not entirely unjustified question in Germany. The discussion eventually escalated into a duel between Pallat and the "capitalist servant" Rolf-Ulrich Kaiser. Pallat accused Kaiser, as an alleged representative of the music industry, of ripping off fans with inflated prices. Kaiser asked back at what price the self-produced and self-distributed Scherben records were sold, and then calculated that the band would make an excellent profit due to their significantly lower costs. Pallat could have replied: okay, there's a fair bit left over, but it ends up in the pockets of the musicians and not the industry. Instead, he promised on camera that the prices were only so high because of the initial investment and that the next editions would of course be significantly cheaper. They weren't.

The programme was broadcast live – and the producers had come up with something special. Monitors were set up in the foyer of a concert by Frumpy, taking place that evening, to broadcast the discussion. A reporter with a microphone was positioned there to relay questions from the audience to the studio. However, the young concertgoers began to engage in lively discussions amongst themselves, rendering the reporter superfluous and seeing through the pop hype (at least as well as the experts invited to the programme). It wasn't just the team in the studio that was far to the left of today's mainstream opinion: the viewers also expressed their perspectives. For example: talking about record prices would be putting the cart before the horse. People need to talk about capitalism, they said, and terms like meritocracy are just a cover-up. They create the illusion that people can get ahead through their own performance, and thus only exacerbate exploitation. It would be better to talk about capitalism – which was shit. The function of concerts was also summarised: People should forget about the working day, and pay for it with the meagre wages they had just earned. Protests would also be integrated into the spiral of exploitation and consumption. Today, one can only marvel at the ease with which words such as capitalism and exploitation slipped from the lips of this random group of young people.

THE ENEMY IN YOUR OWN BED

The dream of being able to earn a living with music often turned out to be just that – a dream. It sounded very nice at first: non-alienated labour, control of the means of production, self-determination. But record contracts were usually to the musicians' disadvantage, and sales figures were limited. In order to have enough gigs, bands were forced to constantly travel from one end of the country to the other. At least the many flat-sharing communities and the rural communes provided a self-help network, which meant that accommodation was taken care of and no additional hotel costs were incurred. There wasn't much money to be made from the concerts, not from commercial organisers anyway. But even the numerous concerts organised by enthusiasts at the time, whose often amateurish organisation caused some problems, were not profitable enterprises. Admission prices were low, and had to be (even The Rolling Stones only charged 6 Deutschmarks admission on their first tour of Germany), because there was no affluent audience. The concert-goers were almost exclusively school kids, apprentices, young workers and students. Those who had to pay the entrance fee from their limited pocket money or modest apprenticeship allowance could not afford to splash out. In addition, there was a consensus within this scene that art and commerce were mutually exclusive. Music should not be a commodity. Pop was almost a dirty word at the time, used to distinguish between "real", "honest", "authentic" music and the musical products with which the industry took back the money its workers had received as wages. At the end of the 1960s, concert organisers had to reckon with concertgoers setting their own entrance fees – at zero. For the audience, the dream of non-alienated labour was translated into "free and outside" – or inside. It almost became a sport to storm concerts or gain entry through back doors or windows. This not only caused problems for the commercial organisers, who were viewed with suspicion as profiteers, but also for the bands, as the threshold up to which admission prices could be charged was low. Or you could put on a free concert, and at least promote yourself and sell your records, if you had any.

By starting their own band, musicians had hoped to cheat capitalism at its own game. Unfortunately, they had brought the enemy into their own bed. It infiltrated your consciousness, because suddenly you had to start doing the calculations. To get to gigs, you needed a band bus. Whereas a few years earlier the beat band had got by borrowing Dad's VW Beetle, now, with the rapidly growing amplifier systems, it had to be at least a Ford Transit. Soon, that was no longer enough. The beat bands had still managed with a few suitcase amplifiers. With the move from small basement clubs, where the audience danced, to large halls, it wasn't just the dancing that was over. The guitar amps became man-sized towers, then a PA was needed to amplify the drums as well – and suddenly the old band bus was too small. It became an endless spiral that was driven more by economic reasons than musical ones. Economically, because the main aim of the development was to provide sound for ever increasing audiences. And also, because the technical upgrading also took place in competition with other groups. But the anti-capitalist audience, determined to storm the concert hall, also judged the bands by their technical equipment. Young men in particular, who dreamed of having their own band, gazed at the gear on display with sparkling eyes. The latter was especially true for electronic bands like Tangerine Dream, where the tech nerds crowded in front of the stage after the performance and whispered mysterious technical terms, brand names and often the purchase prices to each other. Gradually, the music commune and the dream of non-alienated labour had turned into a business enterprise in which people learned to think in terms of investment and profit. This also had an internal effect. The members of the group, which had started out as an egalitarian community, were gradually judged according to performance criteria. "Underachievers" found themselves forced to justify themselves – no longer to a boss, but to their supposed peers. In their book *The New Spirit of Capitalism*, Luc Boltanski and Ève Chiapello describe how the "artist critique" of Fordist capitalism, and its clear hierarchies, became an experimental laboratory for an updated capitalism. In this, Fordist structures, with their discipline on the one hand, and their secure employment relationships and social positions on the other, have been replaced by network-like, project-oriented employment relationships, with seemingly flat hierarchies that mobilise the creativity of employees in order to constantly optimise their own exploitation. If Boltanski and Chiapello are indeed right in their thesis, that the criticism of Fordist capitalism articulated in the 1960s has been incorporated into the renewal of capitalism, then former Scherben manager and ex-Green Party chairwoman Claudia Roth would be an example of the efficiency of this re-education.

THE TRUE, THE BEAUTIFUL, THE GOOD ...

It still took a while before hippie musicians became accountants or Green politicians. At the beginning of krautrock, other tones were struck. In *Was tun?*, one of the numerous left-wing magazines, the musicians from Xhol wrote: "From the Alps to the North Sea, so-called 'progressive pop music' can be heard through huge amplifiers. The hit of the season: 'pop festivals'. Pop festivals, whether free or open air, definitely have a commercial character. (...) The majority of pop music comes from the Anglo-Saxon countries, which have a well-organised music industry. (...) In contrast to this is the music of local groups. (...) In order to preserve the honest message of their music and to maintain the greatest possible independence from the system, they accept financial difficulties." Read from today's perspective, this sounds very much like a regressive criticism of capitalism, according to which Anglo-Saxons only think about money, while Germans indulge in inwardness, the true, the beautiful, the good in their summerhouses. Hopefully that's not what was meant. After all, the English and American bands were the role models to be emulated, and at the same time, seen as victims of commercialism. What the authors of the article probably wanted to point out were the contradictions between "progressive" music and its commercialisation. This contradiction was already clearer in the USA and Great Britain, where an infrastructure had long since developed, from management to service providers such as PA rental firms.

Another reason why the Xhol musicians' contribution is not suitable as a docking point for nationalistic interpretations, is that the alleged difference between German inwardness and Anglo-Saxon pursuit of profit no longer exists. The anti-commercial spirit has long since disappeared from the minds of German musicians. Now, they are offered a music industry that is at least as well organised, for which they can attend a pop academy to learn posing, branding and contract law. "Authentic" is now only used as an advertising slogan. But the long-lost anti-capitalist ethos of the krautrockers seems to be exactly what fascinates British or American musicians about krautrock. Martin Büsser wrote: "Krautrock nostalgia, on the other hand, is much more persistent, as long as it doesn't exhaust itself in a happy rave: it dreams of the ideal of a time in which musical avant-garde, political dissidence and the romanticised ensemble could still form a unity." Rolf-Ulrich Kaiser, the organiser of the *Essen Song Days*, wrote as early as 1970 in *Das Buch der neuen Pop-Musik* in answer to the question "What is German about current pop music?": "As long as such new (German) pop music is not marketed as the super-band music of the record industry, as long as musicians prefer to communicate rather than earn money, it can serve as one of the means of awakening creativity." Whatever is supposed to be specifically German about this, however, remains Kaiser's secret.

In the wake of the krautrock hype, the number of bands categorised as belonging to this genre has grown steadily. Every new book brings to light another name that was either forgotten, or so marginal that there was nothing substantial to forget about anyway. This includes Anima, the duo of Paul and Limpe Fuchs. Paul with various wind instruments (some of which they built themselves), and Limpe, who is still active today as a drummer. They were only accepted into the krautrock canon late on, because the music had nothing to do with rock. Anima played at the same events as the krautrock protagonists – e.g. on the *Underground Explosion* tour in 1969, for which Limpe Fuchs was the poster's main motif. The poster and Anima's performance inspired Der Spiegel to headline its report with "Exhibitionists to the Fore", and to begin with the Munich public order office's requirement that the performers must be "sufficiently clothed": "In particular, the pubic area and buttocks, and in the case of women, also the breasts, must be covered". Nevertheless, Limpe Fuchs performed only with body painting – like on the poster, which accordingly caused offence to the authorities. The duo belonged to the circle of Viennese actionists, and were musically close to what is now known as improv or real-time music, as opposed to free jazz. If you broaden the focus to include the border areas that have little to do with pop music, you will find even more female musicians: e.g. the pianists Irène Schweizer and Donata Höffer. Nicole van den Plas played piano with SvenÅke Johansson and Alfred Harth in the group E.M.T. (Energy/

Movement/Totale). The violinist Madelaine Pütz played with the trio Action Organisation at Zodiak in West Berlin. That's not much, but it's a better balance than when krautrock became mainly rock. Essentially, krautrock was music in which women remained the exception.

In the mid-1960s, pop music was still much more feminine. In the first *Beat-Club* season, women were not only present in the form of presenter Uschi Nerke, but also among the audience. They were not in the role of fans clamouring for redemption, stretching their arms out towards their idol; instead, you see self-confident, well-dressed women dancing and having fun, while the band provides the soundtrack in the background. In comparison, the young men beside them looked rather shy and awkward. In the homeland of beat music, England, the mods' favourite music was American soul – particularly popular were the songs of black girl groups such as The Ronettes, The Marvelettes, or Martha and the Vandellas, whose songs were covered by all the English boys' bands, from The Beatles to The Who. Women were also successful songwriters, such as Carole King, who penned the song "Chains" from the first Beatles album, and was an avowed role model for Lennon and McCartney. And on countless hits from this period, dancers were set in motion to the grooves of bassist Carol Kaye.

What made the music attractive to English youths was the equation of the rigid British class society, against which they rebelled, with segregation in the United States. This made African-American music interesting – and especially that of the girl groups, which embodied a double rebellion. Until then, black women had only appeared in films as cooks or cleaners. If you look at the TV appearances of the girl groups, you see self-confident, well-dressed, sophisticated young women who could have been found working in an advertising agency on New York's Madison Avenue. The enthusiasm and identification with this act of self-empowerment and emancipation, made the sound of the British bands more feminine – the vocal ranges were far above the overtly masculine sound of rock in later years. Fashion for both men and women was also influenced by this, and even the mods' favourite means of transport reflected this development: the round shape of the Italian branded Vespa scooter, which could also be driven while wearing a skirt. In the many rear-view mirrors with which the scooter was overtly adorned, you could not only check the traffic behind you, but above all your own appearance.

Swinging London developed rapidly from mod to hippie – and so did fashion. While the mods still made a clear distinction between men and women, things now became more androgynous. Whether in jeans or kaftans, the boundaries were blurred. This also found resonance in Germany. The provocation of the mods' elegant suits, which took aim at class boundaries, was only partially understood in Germany, where workers and the petty bourgeoisie imitated the upper classes on Sundays. The colourful fashion of the hippies, which blurred gender differences but also had a romantic longing for the Orient, was better received. It coincided with a new set of debates about gender roles and feminism.

The famous flyer by the Women's Council of the SDS (Socialist German Student Union), which showed a woman with an axe, appeared in 1968 and is regarded as the initial spark for the debates within the left-wing movement about feminism. Krautrock was largely indifferent to these debates, which gained momentum from 1968 onwards. After all, it produced hardly any macho poses and slogans; no Mick

Jagger or Jim Morrison. Krautrock, however, was a boys' universe – apparently so exclusive that it could contribute almost nothing to the supreme discipline of the pop song: the love song. Women in krautrock: not much to report. If there were women, they were a huge exception and only in the traditional role of a singer, such as Inga Rumpf in Frumpy or Renate Knaup from Amon Düül. Before the group divided, it followed a collective concept of living and making music together, in which everyone played a part – men and women. However, the only woman the press found worth mentioning was the fashion model Uschi Obermaier, described as a "lascivious rattle-shaking woman". The only role that was really accepted for women was as a vocalist. The one exception was Limpe Fuchs. Yet the restriction to the role of singer was not exclusively a problem relating to krautrock. Things weren't much better elsewhere either. Which is not to say that women didn't play a role. At least in the mid 1960s, they were the most important target group for music. The boys were on stage, but it was the female fans who decided the success or failure of a band. They also had a visual influence on pop music through fashion and design. However, when krautrock entered the stage as a latecomer at the end of the 60s, the joy of fashion was suddenly gone, and was now condemned as "consumerist terror". With the professionalisation and transformation into a rock band, the women disappeared. They only existed in krautrock as the "girlfriend of …" Even when the bands lived together in shared flats or communes, music was a male pursuit. At some point, this led to rebellion in the Scherben, and the women who lived on the band's farm founded their own band, Carambolage. But that was in the early 1980s, in the heyday of punk, when krautrock was already history.

ART & ARTIFICIALITY

After 1945, the visual arts in Germany had a lot of catching up to do in order to reconnect with international developments. Initially, people looked to France, to the abstract paintings of the Informel movement. They signalled a radical break with the highly politicised and nationalistic art of the Nazi era. The authors of the post-war years often pursued a moralising reappraisal of their war experiences, and usually wrote in a formally less avant-garde manner. On the other hand, the visual arts were much more radical in their new beginning, with which they pursued an artistic self-exploration. It not only departed from the forced and politically instrumentalized representationalism of the pre-1945 period, but also distanced itself from the Socialist Realism prescribed in the GDR. From the 1960s onwards, the focus increasingly turned towards the USA and the latest trends in art. Andy Warhol, his paintings and films, as well as the Factory with its staff of artists and freaks, attracted attention. The first film for which Kraftwerk composed the music, was Katharina Sieverding's *Life and Death* in 1969, in which the camera rests on the filmmaker as the main character in long takes. Kraftwerk produced slow-motion drones to accompany the film.

The painters and sculptors had long been dissatisfied: they painted in the seclusion of their studios, at some point the picture was hung in a gallery, and finally, if they were lucky enough to still be alive, the museum came calling. The image of the solitary painter working in the studio, or with an easel in nature, seemed anachronistic in a world of ever-increasing visual stimuli, especially in the face of the flood of images from television, which was pushing its way into the private sphere. While film and photography had already triggered new developments in the visual arts in the 1920s, television now brought images into the home, into everyday life. And so, in the 1960s, the medium of television became a subject of art – from the mere presence of the TV, often stacked dozens of times on top of each other, to the video art of Nam June Paik. But even public television, which is rightly criticised today for being boring, developed an astonishing enthusiasm for experimentation in these years; the visual effects in *Beat-Club* would be the most well known, yet artistically rather harmless example.

In addition to the flood of images, the reaction to everyday culture and its media dissemination brought something else: these mediums were not silent. Sound, whether as environmental noise, voice or music, became a category in which visual artists also began to take an interest. Two contradictory tendencies were present in the DNA of krautrock from the very beginning, among both makers and listeners: on the one hand, the search for new forms of artistic expression beyond the classical boundaries of art genres, and also beyond those between art and everyday life. Many of the first krautrockers were art students, and the first performances often took place as part of art events or in galleries. On the other side was the faction coming from beat or rock music, which denounced art as artificiality and insisted on the alleged authenticity of honest, handmade music. The categorisations were often very arbitrary. The Velvet Underground were more likely to be heard in the art scene: to the ears of rock fans, the band mainly made noise – especially John Cale with the drones he produced on the viola. The categorisation into "authentic" and "inauthentic" seems rather peculiar, because the electrified, advanced blues rock that was considered to be the most authentic was itself highly artificial. The music was a hybrid whose ingredients had crossed the Atlantic several times in both directions: from West Africa and Europe to the USA, where these ingredients blended into blues, rock and roll, and soul; from there to England, where young people, mainly from the working class, transformed this music into beat and psychedelic; and then back to the USA, where the British bands became the blueprint for a legion of garage bands from The Velvet Underground to The New York Dolls and The Ramones – who then once again inspired British punks. It is also strange that the electric guitar and the synthesiser emerge as antipodes in this debate, with the electric guitar being given the seal of approval as authentic. Ten years earlier, things looked very different. Bob Dylan had been booed at the Newport Folk Festival because he had swapped his acoustic guitar for an electric guitar – the folkies saw this as pandering to the culture industry. In the meantime, the electric guitar had been given the seal of authenticity and the synthesiser was a betrayal. Yet both instruments were roughly the same age, created in the first decades of the 20th century when electricity began to be utilised to produce sound. For conservatives, however, the synthesiser was always a symbol of decadence and unmanliness. In *Anders als du und ich*, a film about homosexuals, directed by – of all people – Veit Harlan, the most important propaganda filmmaker of the Nazi era, electronic music stands for a threatening otherness.

In 1969, when the West Berlin Academy of the Arts organised 3 *Nights of Living and Minimal Art*, it became clear just how poorly the claim to art and the wish for authenticity fitted together. According to the announcement, 'Living Music' was to be music that anarchistically broke with the constraints of tradition. The poster announced The Alexis Korner Blues Group, The Donata Höffer Group and The Alexander von

Schlippenbach Nonett with Peter Brötzmann and Manfred Schoof. Authenticity was a notion that both blues and free jazz fans held equally dear – only the two sides didn't necessarily share the same criteria. This led to a dispute between the different groups of spectators at this event, which resulted in damage to the objects in the exhibition in which the concerts took place. The controversy between art, artificiality and (alleged) authenticity lived on in punk. In West Berlin, it escalated when Martin Kippenberger took over the club SO36 and attempted to bring art, in the form of the painting scene baptised as "Neue Wilde", and punk together under one roof. Kippenberger used the result of this attempt in his painting "Dialogue with the Youth of Today". It shows the artist with a thick bandage on his head and wounds he had sustained in a fight at SO36, when punks for whom the beer was too expensive and those who didn't like all that art – or both at the same time – had beaten him up. In the same place, began the path of a band that brought together the seemingly authentic and absolute artificiality – vitalistic hammering and the art figure Blixa Bargeld: Einstürzende Neubauten. The hammer had previously been used in Schnitzler's Zodiak or with Faust. In general, some of the punk and new wave sounds were quite reminiscent of psychedelic and krautrock. But you weren't allowed to say that out loud, because the image of punk was: there was nothing before us. At most, stoned hippies. The British punks, on the other hand, admitted to listening to Faust, Can, Kraftwerk, Neu or Cluster.

REBIRTH OF GERMANY

David Stubb's book, published in 2014, is titled *Future Days: Krautrock and the Building of Modern Germany*. The BBC had already broadcast a documentary entitled *Krautrock – The Rebirth of Germany* in 2009. The alleged contribution of krautrock to this rebirth went largely unnoticed in Germany for a rather long time. The British understanding of Germany's previous rebirths has not been the best: from the national unification movement in the 19th century to National Socialism, the notion of the rebirth of the German nation has always been the domain of the right-wing. In the case of krautrock, the "rebirth" claimed by the BBC is said to have been the achievement of a rather small handful of bands. But any reference to the nation can at most be found in the political rockers such as Floh de Cologne, Ton Steine Scherben or Checkpoint Charlie. Yet although they sang in German, German identity was certainly not their concern. At most it was as a negation: "It's not this country" (Scherben). Whenever they had to deal with the nation state, it was in the form of the police.

In 1974, *Autobahn*, Kraftwerk's fourth album, marked the beginning of the band's transformation into man-machine, the transformation of musicians into robots. If this was intended as a commentary on Germany's rebirth, then it is also a metaphor for the transformation of the Germans into industrious monads who, free of empathy, now turned the wheels in favour of the economic miracle instead of military victory. There is hardly any explanatory help from the band itself in the form of interviews. One exception is a conversation that Ralf Hütter had with the American music journalist Lester Bangs during their first US tour in 1975: "After the war,

German entertainment was destroyed. The German people were robbed of their culture, putting an American head on it. I think we are the first generation born after the war to shake this off, and know where to feel American music and where to feel ourselves."

So the murmur of national identity is there after all – and in Germany, this apparently only exists in the role of victim? Whereby the destruction of German culture had already taken place before 1945, and was carried out by the Germans themselves with great and often deadly zeal? After this interview, Kraftwerk went back into silence. So one can only speculate or refer to the image that the band has created for itself. It suggests: "robots don't eat sauerkraut". The supposedly most German of all dishes, and source of the derogatory label of "krauts", doesn't taste good to them. In general, Kraftwerk's play with German-ness, the supposedly typical German coolness and effectiveness, is always broken and ironic. This distinguishes them from the one-dimensional Teutonic rock of Rammstein. You won't find a Reichsparteitag backdrop with pyrotechnics and light domes or a recourse to Leni Riefenstahl's aesthetics with Kraftwerk. Instead, the band quotes classical modernism in its appearance, cover art and stage presentation. Above all, however, Kraftwerk differ from the musical representatives of "we're not right-wing, but ..." in one crucial respect: they are completely un-manly. Yet masculinity – either threatened or martial, always ready to use violence – is the obsession around which all right-wing or fascist ideas have revolved around since the end of the 19th century. In 1920, Hans Pfitzner's pamphlet *Die neue Aesthetik der Impotenz* (The New Aesthetics of Impotence) was published in opposition to Schönberg and New Music. Pfitzner had already warned of the "Futurist danger" in 1917. In his book, he saw Germany threatened by "pacifism", a "flood of jazz" and "atonal Americanism".

Have the Germans, as Hütter said in the interview with Lester Bangs, had an "American head" screwed onto them, and then forced the unfortunate Hütter to emulate American idols on the Hammond organ? Was American culture forced on all Germans? Large sections of the middle classes took a very similar view after 1945. With the loss of cultural hegemony, they also lost part of the legitimisation of their claim to power, both internally and externally. Defeated by the Americans, of all people, who – according to the conviction of the educated middle classes – only had chewing gum instead of culture. In the 1950s, there were actually plans to thank the Americans with "cultural packages" for the care and food packages the USA had supplied the Germans with after the war. The left also joined in the chorus about the cultureless Americans, as did official GDR cultural policy, which had misunderstood Adorno's concept of the culture industry and believed that German handiwork was superior to American mass culture, as it was deeply rooted in German identity.

Krautrock historiography usually ignores the social origins of the protagonists. In the beginning, rock and roll was mainly a proletarian pastime. If you wanted to listen to this music, you had to go to the carnivals, where the lowlifes hung out, or to bars of rather ill repute. The same applied to British beat music. You could find it in Hamburg's Reeperbahn, in Berlin pubs or in working-class neighbourhoods like Neukölln. During the first rock and roll riots in 1958 on the occasion of Bill Haley's tour, there was only one high school student among the arrested youths who had to cool off after the endless melodious sound of the opening band – swing with the Kurt Edelhagen Orchestra – and a 15-minute show by

Bill Hailey. Everyone else was a labourer or apprentice. When Jerry Lee Lewis hammered his "Great Balls of Fire" into the piano at the Starclub in 1962, the Hamburger Abendblatt wrote with a sneer: "The young people, some of them very young, are machine workers, apprentices, industrial trainees, dock workers – simple, undemanding, strong." It took a while for the young bourgeoisie to acquire a taste for the forbidden fruit and venture into places like the Starclub. Previously, the children of the middle classes had listened to Bach and Mozart or, if they wanted to demonstrate progressiveness, cultivated jazz and French chanson. This could be defended to the conservative authorities as a different, more modern form of art music. Listening to guitar noise from English or American bands, on the other hand, was a radical break from tradition.

Hütter and Schneider came from upper middle class backgrounds. They met at the music academy, a place where back then you probably wouldn't have found children from working class households with a magnifying glass. It is therefore almost a provocation of their milieu of origin, that the two of them described themselves as "music workers" at some point. They were certainly familiar with the discourse surrounding cultural aspirations and Americanisation, as the German middle classes were especially divided on this issue. The conservatives – whose concept of the cultural nation had something exclusionary, anti-Western and anti-democratic about it from the outset – were on the defence due to their liaison with National Socialism, even if they pretended nothing had happened when meeting in Bayreuth to the sounds of Wagner. On the other hand, there were the younger people and the up-and-comers. For them, turning to modernism was also a means of fighting their way out of old structures and against the holders of the positions they were pushing for. Abstract painting, the latest French or Italian films, French philosophers and American jazz became a sign of modernity.

Towards the end of the 1960s, an unusual coalition was formed: young workers joined forces with the equally ambitious middle class in their fight against authoritarian structures. In the cultural field, they came together in pop music, which within a few years had gone from being purely dance music to something more and more sophisticated, without becoming too domesticated. Without this rare, cross-class coalition, combined with a unique generational conflict, the major changes in West Germany from the end of the 1960s to the end of the 1970s would certainly not have taken place in this form – in other words, almost everything that is summarised under the cipher "'68". With the end of the post-war boom, marked by the 1973 oil crisis, this coalition fell apart again. Three decades later, following intensifying struggles over distribution, the nation was rediscovered as the cement for a society that was drifting further and further apart. This new nation would like to be a pop nation and world export champion, also in the field of pop culture. German musicians are making their contribution to this, but in addition to current music production, there is obviously also a need for something like a pop history to call their own. This also explains the late awakening of German interest in krautrock. Frank Apunkt Schneider writes on the transformation of pop in Germany from a project of self-reeducation to a national soundtrack: "In the end, pop became German after all. But as Germans are, of course, that doesn't work in the form of dual citizenship. It has to be completely German, right down to the bone, and strip away everything foreign, dazzling, incomprehensible or mysterious ..." Luckily, krautrock has produced so much that is abundantly incomprehensible that it will hopefully not be quite so easy to appropriate.

KRAUTROCK FOREVER

The next youth movement came at the end of the 1970s, and once again it came from the UK: punk. In contrast to the optimistic 1960s, the social climate had cooled considerably. No future. What distinguished British punks from German punks: musicians like Johnny Rotten drew on krautrock, especially Can. Faust, with their proto-industrial sound, were a source of inspiration for bands like Cabaret Voltaire. What made the krautrockers interesting was that they never got caught up in the commercialisation machine. This was interpreted as honesty and loyalty to principle, although in reality it was probably more due to a lack of opportunity. Krautrock had also retained the appeal of otherness, in a country where The Beatles had become national saints after whom airports were later named. German punks mostly ignored the British musicians' praise for the krautrockers. They were lumped together with hippies and old '68ers – both dirty words. One would think that the krautrockers' ideas of independence, refusal of commerce and do-it-yourself ethos might have appealed to the punks. But the '68ers had embarked on a march through the institutions. The result was, instead of a change in these institutions, a change in those who marched. The bourgeois segment of the '68ers had eventually become ordinary citizens, who now faced the next generation as social workers, teachers or professors.

The fact that people in England are more interested in krautrock today than ever before, decades after its almost unnoticed disappearance, can be partly explained by the longing for a pop music that does not yet seem to obey the rules of the new capitalism as a start-up or freelance corporation. However, the gap between desire and reality is irrelevant. It is precisely because krautrock was so marginal that it remains suited to such dreams. In Germany, there are less pleasant reasons to remember krautrock. In this country, the memory serves to construct a national pop history, the message of a cool Germany that has learnt from its history. But why are musicians around the world still interested in krautrock – 50 years after the little-noticed and relatively short-lived scene in Germany disappeared from existence? Krautrock didn't even need to disappear from the charts. It had never made it there – the only exception was Can with the theme music for one of the then successful TV thrillers based on stories by Francis Durbridge. And perhaps Kraftwerk – but only after krautrock had long since passed.

One reason for the interest in krautrock is precisely its widespread failure, which gives krautrock the aura of the uncorrupted. Krautrock has been spared commercialisation and the flattening into stadium rock. It has also (so far) been spared the zombie existence of revival tours or appearances in golden oldie shows. The krautrockers are glorified as people who simply did their thing, unwavering and immune to all pressure to conform and bend for commercial success. They appear as an alternative to a thoroughly economised world that only gives musicians the choice between adaptation, defensive complaining or cynical realism. The longing for krautrock is the longing for a capitalism which people still believed was possible to leave; whose table was so richly laid that even for those who refused it, there was still enough left to pursue their dream of a different life on a farm somewhere, or in a niche in the city.

This also applies to Kraftwerk, even if at first glance their cool technical efficiency seems to be quite different from the wanderlust of the world musicians of Embryo or the harsh sounds of Kluster. Kraftwerk are a reminder of the seemingly functional capitalism of the 1950s and 1960s, when achievement was worthwhile, and you had a job, prospects in life, advancement and security seemed guaranteed. A place where people did not defend the Biedermeier era, but wanted modern cities with modern architecture that promised a better life for everyone.

FUTURE DAYS

In England, the longing for a future that has not materialised is perhaps a bigger issue, because the development from a social democratic state to a (seemingly) deregulated, neoliberal state with all its consequences for the individual has progressed further. A process that Margaret Thatcher had begun by disempowering the trade unions was accelerated once again by New Labour under Tony Blair. The hopeful "Friday on my Mind" (Easybeats) of the 1960s becomes meaningless if you have to work a second job at the weekend in order to somehow pay the rent. Not to mention cultural production. Mark Fisher writes in *Ghosts of My Life*: "Despite all its rhetoric of novelty and innovation, neoliberal capitalism has gradually but systematically deprived artists of the resources necessary to produce the new. In the UK, the postwar welfare state and higher education maintenance grants constituted an indirect source of funding for most of the experiments in popular culture between the 1960s and the 80s. The subsequent ideological and practical attack on public services meant that one of the spaces where artists could be sheltered from the pressure to produce something that was immediately successful was severely circumscribed."

The longing for a time when the future was still something to hope for has since spawned its own genre of music in the UK under the term hauntology, with bands such as The Focus Group, The Advisory Circle and Belbury Poly often using old black and white footage from the childhood days of television in their videos. Simon Reynolds writes about hauntology in *Retromania*, the book in which he explores retro loops and cultural stasis: "The UK hauntologists are self-consciously playing with a set of bygone cultural forms that lie outside the post-Elvis/Beatles rock and pop mainstream, stuff that was either pre-rock'n'roll or that remained outside rock'n'roll. They conjure a Britain unaffected by Americanisation." That sounds a little strange – Britain had become the centre of the pop world in the 1960s and 1970s precisely because of its creative appropriation of American music. The sometimes simple inability of German bands to cope with the imported rock forms is misunderstood as an alternative to Americanisation. This Americanisation is also seen as the cause of the destruction of the British welfare state. Here, too, Germany serves as a counter-model. In his krautrock history *Future Days*, David Stubbs creates an image of Germany that seems to come from an SPD election campaign brochure more than four decades old. A country where the trains run on time, and workers and employers are united in a cosy social partnership. "A 'model state' might be an exaggeration, but there is a case to be made that of all the world's major social democracies, it is the least worst state. Unlike the UK, it has retained its manufacturing base and has a relatively healthy dialogue between management and unions, whose workers enjoy a sensible and well-funded work-life balance. Unlike the UK, there is a sane attitude towards housing, with renting the norm and no ridiculous boom-and-bust property market. Its artists enjoy generous cultural endowments, every major city boasts superb galleries and arts facilities, transport networks thrum with functionality ..." Elsewhere, Stubbs provides a biographical explanation of his fascination with krautrock: while his schoolmates brought their Slayer records to school, he arrived with a Faust record. The outsider for whom "German otherness" (Stubbs) became a point of escape. Here, the mechanism that made young Germans reach for English records in the 1960s has apparently been reversed.

Kraftwerk remains the German band that is most frequently mentioned when today's musicians refer to krautrock. The question as to why this is the case is: is it merely name-dropping, a misunderstanding – or something more? One reason has already been given: Kraftwerk as a symbol of longing for a modernity with its promises that did not materialise. A modern age in which Thatcher would serve customers in a friendly manner in her parents' grocery shop, and in which Harold Wilson's talk of the "white heat" of the technological revolution would actually have led to a prosperous Britain. But there is also the dystopian reversal of Kraftwerk's "friendly modernity". Bands like New Order also refer to Kraftwerk. Because of the subjectively perceived coldness of their music, and the emotionless delivery of their lyrics, Kraftwerk seem to symbolise a world in which interpersonal communication has broken down. Avant-garde, a term that inevitably appears in every article about Kraftwerk, had become associated with stagnation and depression. It seems to be a quality of the band: to allow such contradictory interpretations. However, one should not attach too much importance to the labels assigned by music journalism. Kraftwerk and futurism, for example – Kraftwerk's friendly future has nothing whatsoever to do with the disruptive, violence-glorifying futurism of Tommaso Marinetti, the author of the *Manifesto del Futurismo* of 1909 and follower of Mussolini. Nor do Kraftwerk have anything to do with the ever-invoked closeness to the Düsseldorf art scene and its forefather Joseph Beuys. Beuys' esotericism, grease and felt are diametrically opposed to Kraftwerk's smooth, metallic aesthetic. In the organicism of Joseph Beuys there is always a longing for decay. "Everyone is an artist" is the often-quoted saying from Joseph Beuys. Perhaps this is true – but he remained the professor with a pension entitlement. He wasn't inclined to share that. In contrast, Kraftwerk's self-stylisation as "music workers" is much more democratic – even if that sounds a little strange given the social class that Schneider and Hütter come from. Worker means that the necessary skills can be learnt, like plumber or electrician.

The longing for a modern, European Germany perhaps has another reason. Florian Schneider's mother had experienced the dark side of Germany first-hand during the Third Reich. Evamaria Schneider-Esleben was considered half-Jewish according to Nazi racial doctrine. Her mother did everything she could to conceal her origins, but lived in constant fear of being discovered. The people's radio receiver – also known as the "Goebbels snout" after the Nazi propaganda minister – on the cover of "Radioactivity" thus takes on a subtext that can only be guessed at. Florian Schneider and Ralf Hütter always hid behind their work. And even then they remained taciturn.

At first glance, it seems strange that Kraftwerk, of all bands, have become "the" blueprint for what krautrock is, as they are so different from the mainstream of the German music scene. It is their artificiality that makes them a surface of projection for other musicians with very different backgrounds. And – although a male band – also for female musicians. Kraftwerk are as far removed from ostentatious rock machismo as they are from the self-pity of the eternally misunderstood man. They are robots. The modern housewife knows all about them – from hoovers to microwaves. Ladytron is an example of this. At the same time, their song "Seventeen" is also an example of the dystopian reinterpretation of Kraftwerk. The video is more reminiscent of the BDM, the youth organisation for female youth during the Nazi era, than of women freed from tedious housework by modern technology. Even before an androgynous image was accepted in pop music, Ralf Hütter and Florian Schneider recorded the soundtrack to Katharina Sieverding's 1969 film "Life & Death" about a queer search for identity.

It would be surprising if, over the years of the band's existence, the social changes were not reflected in the music and, very importantly for Kraftwerk, the presentation. The friendly "music workers" of the Ralf and Florian period have become the unapproachable "human machines" of their latest concerts. You can admire them, but they can also be feared, which reflects the ambiguity of the digitalisation of the world. With this message, Kraftwerk appear conservative at a time when millions of people are using social media.

The reception of music is always dependent on social circumstances and their changes, as well as the individual circumstances and experiences of the listener. In addition, since the beginning of the 20th century, composition and performance for recorded sound, and the consumption of the music reproduced in this way, have both diverged in time. The repeated playing of the sound carriers in different situations makes their meaning fluid – whatever the original idea of the musicians was. Music has had to live with this risk since the invention of the record. Whereby the real risk is not the changing reception with different social conditions, but the loss of meaning through endless repetition. Such reinterpretation does not only happen to music. It also happens in the opposite direction. In the 1920s – until its closure by the Nazis in 1933 – the Bauhaus was an art school that aimed to create an affordable, practical and beautiful living environment for everyone, from everyday objects and graphic design to architecture. Why a British goth band named itself after it, and turned the film actor Bela Lugosi into the undead in its best-known song, is a mystery. For Kraftwerk, on the other hand, the Bauhaus movement was the source of inspiration for their corporate identity. And the link to the Bauhaus is also an unspoken political statement. Kraftwerk wanted to continue where the Bauhaus had to stop in 1933: a democratic society in which the good things, the good life, are accessible to everyone. Kraftwerk themselves contributed to the interpretability of their pieces. On *Radioactivity*, the ambivalence of radioactivity as either the radio (the cover) or radioactivity (nuclear energy and Madame Curie), eventually became unambiguous by listing the place names of reactor accidents.

Music can be a seismograph that does more than just indicating visible social developments. This seismograph can also indicate future developments that are still barely perceptible. When dystopian sounds were heard in the heyday of krautrock in the early 1970s, it was a warning that the future might not be as friendly as the music-making hippies in the rural commune had hoped. In addition to the fear of the apocalypse of nuclear war, it was above all the concern about a future for which George Orwell had provided the blueprint in his book *1984*. The reception focussed on the surveillance state described by Orwell. The importance of control over language and knowledge of history described in the book only came into focus later. The other vision of the future, in which Aldous Huxley depicts a consumer society organised by estates in a permanent drug frenzy, did not seem so threatening at first. Only a few people thought that the two futures, which at first glance appear so different, were not an 'either/or' proposition, but this now seems quite likely. And wasn't the "cosmic courier's" friendly packaging of civilisation fatigue, often combined with a longing for a mystically transfigured Orient, also a dystopia? Criticising the dystopian turn in the interpretation of krautrock as a falsification of a somehow conceived "real" krautrock, makes little sense in view of the seismographic abilities of music. Instead, one should discuss which developments have caused this shift, and where in krautrock there could be a utopian moment that counteracts the resignation to these developments.

Referring to Kraftwerk as a role model became inflationary at some point. When viewed in the light of day, however, it was often just a case of copying the technical means. It is often overlooked how socio-economic conditions influence musical practice. Music often appears to be an act of pure will. You just have to want it – which, when seen in the light of day, is the credo of neoliberalism. In the 1960s/1970s, rents were still priced so that young people could afford their own flat when they came of age. Finding a rehearsal room for a band was reasonably affordable. And rooms for clubs where bands could perform were also affordable. Students didn't leave university in debt for the rest of their lives. Wages were enough to survive without a full-time job if you weren't too demanding. There was still time for music. Those who were even more modest could survive without a job. The social security systems were still intact. Those who had a job were still used to working collectively, instead of an isolated existence as a clickworker in a home office. This created the social skills needed to play in a band based on the division of labour. Land speculation, deindustrialisation and the conversion to a service economy with its Mc-Jobs – all with the active help of both right-wing and left-wing governments – have destroyed the conditions that bands needed. You listened to Kraftwerk with electronic percussion instruments and thought: great, you can do that with headphones and rehearse in your bedroom. Soon the equipment was programmable. One push of a button and the technology delivered beats without deviation or fatigue. The next step was MIDI and the ability to operate all the instruments on your own, without any annoying debates with your bandmates. Anyway, you would first have to find those bandmates: at least three real friends and not just Twitter followers. At the end of this chain is the laptop artist, who dozes behind his laptop and reads his emails during his gigs.

A band like Tangerine Dream has gone all the way from concepts borrowed from the avant-garde and free improvisation, via the synthesiser instead of the laptop, where musicians sit on stage as if they were in their home office. They have thus become a blueprint for the disappearance of music as social interaction. On the other hand, there are bands that refer to Faust, Neu! or Can – as "musicians' musicians" with more influence within the music scene than with the general public. And no matter how similar these newer bands sound to their older role models – the claimed role model function is true in one respect: it is the joy of playing together. The second influential band from the krautrock universe is Can. Their largely improvised music brought back humanity. The break with the conventions of pop music is also musically much more radical than with Kraftwerk. Visually, Can remained the classic rock quintet with guitar, bass, keyboard, drums and a singer as frontman. Even if Can doesn't have the guitar hero endlessly strumming his guitar with the right facial expressions, they developed something like a collective virtuosity. If something is emphasised by the musicians who cite Can as a role model, it is usually the drumming of Jaki Liebezeit. The description then revolves around terms such as "motorik" or "monotonous" to make Liebezeit one of the founding fathers of techno – something that Kraftwerk were not spared. But that is probably a misunderstanding. In an obituary on the occasion of Liebezeit's death in 2017 by Ulrich Stock for Zeit Online, there is little enthusiasm from the drummer for the monotonous 4/4 beat. For Liebezeit, it is "the rhythm of Christianity, of crucifixion" and "the normality that exists here".

Can's studio is now on display at the Rock & Pop Museum in Gronau. Kraftwerk have also come to rest in the museum alongside other artefacts of a modernity that is no longer modern, in a decontextualised collection of artworks that have simply been left over after the "end of history" (as proclaimed by Francis Fukuyama), and only attract attention when they go under the hammer at Sotheby's as a profitable investment. The esoteric aspect of krautrock, on the other hand, has not ended up in the museum. It continues in wellness music and dark wave. Today, rural communes are founded successfully by nationalistic settlers in areas where they can swim as freely as fish in water with their hateful ideology. Although this is not the fault of krautrock, it shows that some ideas from its heyday are not automatically avant-garde in the sense of being an emancipatory project. The protagonists of the new capitalism, whether from Apple or Google, also came from the hippie flat share. The political personnel in Germany, who have started a race to catch up in the competition between capitalist nations through the "Agenda" policy, come from a similar socialisation; at least as far as the Greens are concerned. They started out as an alternative and ended up with "there is no alternative".

Currently, the most successful music export from Germany is the biggest conceivable opposite to Kraftwerk: Rammstein. Instead of the friendly Germany of Kraftwerk travelling to Paris on the Transeuropa Express for a shopping spree, the Wehrmacht boot is once again trampling everything underfoot, paying homage to a barbaric cult of masculinity, for which sex is just a bodily function like digestion. It's all just art, just satire, say their defenders. That may be true for some viewers. For them, a concert by the band is like going to the cinema to see a splatter film. But you shouldn't be quite so sure. Anyone who has ever sat on the S-Bahn with fans on their way back from a Rammstein concert, wonders whether everyone believes that this is just satire.

In contrast, Kraftwerk's friendly Keynesian capitalism remains rational, a human endeavour, even if its rationality never worked out that way in reality. It is the longing for a future that was promised but never materialised. It's still better than the whispering of cosmic forces that exaggerate social conditions into eternal principles to which one can only submit – and if it hurts, a bit of yoga can help. The late work of Tangerine Dream, or the records of Klaus Schulze, provide the appropriate soundtrack with spiritually exaggerated bombast and mysterious murmurs. What remains is the forgotten segment of krautrock, the "totally free music". It exists cheerfully under many names: free jazz, improv, sound art, circuit bending, noise (where it's not just meant to show how much boys can stand), Niemandsmusik, real-time music. These scenes contain both the joy of experimentation and the anti-commercial ethos of the krautrockers.

Isolated West Berlin was home to the Zodiak Free Arts Lab, and bands like Kluster and Tangerine Dream, in the late 60s. It was relatively easy to find a flat or a space for artistic experimentation in the city, which was suffering from a population decline that the government was endeavouring to compensate for with financial aid and the expansion of the universities. This was repeated when the two divided halves of the city came together again in 1989 with the end of the GDR. The old centre on the eastern side had been neglected by the GDR government. There was a lot of vacant space where you could find a flat quickly and cheaply – if you didn't require any comfort. But there were also vacant former commercial premises where artistic projects could be realised, and which could be used as event spaces. It was not only the techno scene that developed there. Less noticed, because it was commercially uninteresting, a scene of experimental music also emerged, whose protagonists covered the spectrum from free jazz, to new music and noise. As there was no money to be made, the musicians often rehearsed in their own homes and the venues were often located in residential buildings, a quiet music was created for which the term "Berlin reductionism" was coined at some point. It was so quiet that the fridge at the makeshift bar had to be switched off during performances because its humming was distracting. It was a musical "Arte Povera" that worked with an absolute minimum of resources. In krautrock, which emerged in West Germany during the years of the economic miracle, the question was: who has the biggest drum kit? Now the question was: who has the smallest drum kit? At some point – when a website was set up to announce concerts – it became necessary to find a term for this music.

A number of suggestions circulated until someone raised their finger and said: what we do is compose in real time. Thus the term real-time music was born. What real-time music has in common with much of what was happening in the most experimental and radical segment of krautrock – groups like Kluster or the first records of the successor band Cluster – is the desire to experiment, to improvise and to ignore conventions. Whereby the word improvisation is ambiguous. It can also mean trying something out, and finding something useful by chance – or not. Karlheinz Stockhausen had already resisted this interpretation of the term, making it clear that even where the progression of a piece is not fixed, the musical event is based on a clear idea.

In the meantime, Berlin has followed the path of all metropolises. Progressive gentrification means that the scope for non-commercial art is dwindling. Relatively generous funding from the city, and other cultural institutions, is still helping to keep the real-time music scene alive in the knowledge that tourism is the last growth industry in a largely deindustrialised city. However, this non-commercial scene is a niche. It lives with the risk that in times of tight budgets, the financial support of such niches is the first thing to go. Subsidisation is not without risk either. At a time when a state minister of culture appointed by the Green Party is calling for a "green culture", there is a great temptation to write exact keywords that the ministry wants to hear into the funding applications.

In the age of the Easy Jet, national origin no longer plays a role. This scene is internationally networked, and has thus achieved something that the krautrockers had dreamed of 50 years earlier: that everything German has been stripped away.

In the press release on Faust's move to Virgin Records, the music is described as "rootless", as a product of a modern, urban industrial society. This distance from tradition and being stuck in a cultural identity still makes krautrock interesting today, even if the quantitative contribution to the back catalogue of pop culture is minor. Added to this is the attempt to combine a different life with a different music. Music in Germany in the 1960s made a contribution as a kind of do-it-yourself reeducation. The musical rebels of that time did not change the world, but they did help to turn fascist Germany into a normal, western democracy. What still makes the radical aspects of krautrock interesting today, is the attempt to allow the utopia of a world free of domination to shine through in the music. The question of "right" or "wrong" in music contained the question of the "right" or "wrong" in society. If the reference to krautrock is to be more than just name-dropping or a marketing label, it would have to continue with exactly that spirit.

AGREE TO DISAGREE

A selected Krautrock discography
commented by Holger Adam

Krautrock, what is it anyway? A genre, a derogative term, a song by Faust, ... or: a welcome (and recurring) opportunity to talk about all of this. The music associated with the term in question has eagerly been canonized. From the enthusiastic and idiosyncratic ramblings of Julian Cope's "Krautrocksampler" to encyclopaedic approaches like Alan and Stephen Freeman's "Crack in the Cosmic Egg", there are plenty of books to read and lists to discuss: Who's in, who isn't? Either way, never ending quarrels and disputes surrounding the music and the terms "krautrock" and "kosmische musik" are a testament to their ongoing relevance and fascination. I won't get into the weeds discussing how to separate one from the other, you've just finished a book tackling some of the questions involved in that. If you're still curious though, go on, read more about it, get involved and dig into the list following this short introduction. Said list is not meant to be definitive. It is one possible variant of many and was compiled with only one rule in mind: just one record by each project/band to allow for more variety overall. So, "Monster Movie" is missing, for example. Lists are the result of a selection process; naturally, something will be missing and left out. That said, the list is meant to inspire repeated or further listening, to spark discussions and – potentially – to provoke new lists, perhaps your own! It's all part of the fun. Music is made for enjoyment in the first and for a friendly debate in the second place, after all.

A.R. & Machines: Echo (Polydor, 1972)
Achim Reichel was fronting the Rattles and supporting the Rolling Stones on tour when his promising beat-career ended with a draft for compulsory military service in the Bundeswehr. Returning to music afterwards, he released "Die Grüne Reise" and "Echoes", the latter arguably being his most ambitious work. A delayed-guitar-and-pounding-drums driven psychedelic instrumental double LP, stylistically following the sonic landscape of the first Ash Ra Tempel and predating Göttsching's "Inventions for Electric Guitar". Unfortunately, "Echoes" has never been reissued on vinyl since its initial release in 1972.

Agitation Free: Malesch (Vertigo, 1972)
Back then, and on invitation of the German Goethe-Institut, the Berlin based band travelled parts of Southern Europe, the Middle East and Northern Africa to play several shows and record on site. The collected material would later be used for the band's debut album. The overall breezy and dreamy atmosphere of the music perfectly captures the escapist spirit and wanderlust of the post-WW-II youth in Germany.

Amon Düül: Paradieswärts Düül (Ohr, 1971)
"Paradieswärts Düül" is the work of passionate dilettantes. Compared to all the other records released under the Amon Düül moniker, this album stands out as less chaotic

and noisy but remains as musically limited and sparsely arranged. Its aesthetic naivety and pure-hearted approach make it a charming document of its time. Just sing along: "Love is Peace, Freedom is Harmony", and keep on dreaming.

Amon Düül II: Phallus Dei
(Liberty, 1969)
Amon Düül II, the more professional and long-lived follow-up to Amon Düül. The record is a historical cornerstone, a blueprint for what a psychedelic jam rock band can achieve – from the swirling crescendo of the opening track "Kanaan" right up to today.

Anima-Sound: Stürmischer Himmel
(Ohr, 1971)
The duo's debut stands, like all their recorded music, apart from its krautrock contemporaries. From early on, their unique mix of field-recordings and improvised music on mostly self-built instruments was beyond the rock n roll roots of most krautrock bands. Inspired by Jungian psychology and avant-garde composing techniques, Anima-Sound set out to get away as far as they possibly could from aesthetic formalism and society's restrictions in general – and they made it quite far, indeed.

Annexus Quam: Osmose (Ohr, 1970)
A sonically progressive and jazz-tinged record. The rich instrumentation (including electric organ, recorders, clarinet, saxophone and trombone) provides an almost fusion-like feeling to most of the compositions, foreshadowing something in the vein of Volker Kriegel's "Missing Link" record which would be released two years later.

Ash Ra Tempel: Ash Ra Tempel (Ohr, 1971)
One of the undisputed heavy-weights, undoubtedly. The album consists of two side-long tracks (or shall we say trips) whose musical recipe was often copied but rarely reproduced to similarly stunning results as the legendary power-trio's debut recordings. While Klaus Schulze's drumming is as powerful as a hammer hitting the titular "Amboss", Hartmut Enke's bass is pounding and Manuel Göttsching's guitar wails and echoes back and forth. After flipping the record, "Traummaschine" wobbles as dark and dreamy as it gets.

Between: And Then Waters Opened (Vertigo, 1973)
For decades the ensemble's name proved to ring true. Drawing from musical traditions from all over the world, contemporary jazz as well as minimal music and the inclusive ideas of Carl Orff, their musical variety made Between literally sit

in between genres. They were defying easy categorisation and therefore fell through the cracks. The group's music was neither canonised as krautrock nor recognised as modern classical music. German composer Peter Michael Hamel, the main force behind the project, suffered a similar fate. Decried and derided in his home country as a new age musician, it took some time and avid record collectors to dig Between's music out of the dollar-bins and rescue it from falling into oblivion.

Can: Ege Bamyasi (United Artists Records, 1972)
Another classic and maybe the most balanced and refined of the albums recorded with Damo Suzuki – and the first at Can's own Inner Space Studio. It's groovy, focused and for all its elusive qualities never sounds off-kilter – a masterclass in carefully edited experimentation, but you already knew this, didn't you?

Cluster: Cluster 71 (Philips, 1971)
To put it short: This is proto-industrial-music. Noises emanating from machines that weren't even meant to be musical instruments in the first place. An adventurous approach to organise cacophonous dark matter.
In its calmer moments, Cluster's sonic landscapes evoke the musical tropes of dark ambient, long before this hybrid genre of industrial and ambient music is invented. A brilliant record.

The Cosmic Jokers: The Cosmic Jokers (Kosmische Musik, 1974) Whatever the musicians involved may think of these recordings – they were most likely released by Rolf-Ulrich Kaiser without their consensus –, they stand the test of time as being utterly *out there*. The "Galactic Joke" results in "Cosmic Joy". Millions of kraut-heads can't be wrong.

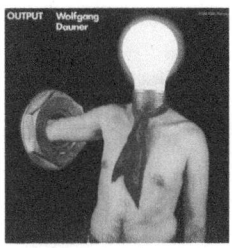

Wolfgang Dauner: Output (ECM Records, 1970) A psychedelic free-form/free jazz album and an early and rather odd entry in the ECM-catalogue. Nonetheless a top-notch crazy sounding record – and a Nurse with Wound list contender for a reason! Eberhard Weber at his most abrasive, Dauner playing piano and keyboards in a Sun Ra style and some fierce 'n fiery free jazz drumming by Fred Braceful! Excellent.

Deuter: D (Kuckuck, 1971) Bedroom-psychedelia by a shy weirdo (see front- and back-cover of the record). Not too soon after, Georg Deuter would become a devoted follower of Bhagwan Shree Rajneesh Osho and relocate to the USA in the mid-1980s, where he resides to this day as a new age musician / healing music practitioner in Santa Fe, New Mexico. His first record, Deuter playing all instruments himself in a very hands-on, kraut-y manner, is very different from all music he would record later and a fun listen in its light-hearted and freewheeling eclecticism.

Thomas Dinger: Für Mich (Telefunken, 1982)
Klaus Dinger's younger brother contributed to the third Neu! record and was a member of La Düsseldorf before leaving, allegedly due to frustration, to record his sole album as a solo artist. With its motoric sensibilities, a track like "Für Dich" (i.e. "For you" – possibly a nod to his brother?) is very much reminiscent of the aforementioned musical projects, but the overall mood of Thomas Dinger's only solo record is rather melancholy and almost gothic in comparison, like-minded to electronic music styles of the time such as minimal- and cold-wave.

Embryo: Rocksession (Brain, 1973)
Even though they explored and incorporated elements from traditional non-western musical styles in their music from early on, Embryo have always been a jazz/fusion band, and they still are (especially after Christian Burchard's daughter Maja took over), but they never sounded smoother and tighter than on the electric piano and organ driven "Rocksession". The record documents the closest Embryo would get to Passport (whose Jimmy Jackson plays on this record) and fusion legends like The Weather Report.

Eno Moebius Roedelius: After the Heat (Sky Records, 1978)
The second collaborative record from the Cluster duo and Brian Eno. The music anticipates the melodic sensibilities of Eno's and Roedelius' later solo works, touches on bits of Harmonia and pairs it here and there (on"Foreign Affairs" and "The Belldog", for example) with a slightly colder touch (which I would attribute to Moebius for good measure). Holger Czukay plays bass on the last track, too!

Eroc: Eroc (Brain, 1975)
Joachim Ehrig's first solo record stylistically is a radical departure from his band Grobschnitt. As an outlet for sonic experimentation with various electronic devices and studio equipment, the tracks on "Eroc" are for the most part stripped off classic rock instrumentation. Most notably the spoken word collage "Horrorgoll" sounds like a Dadaist poem that could have been recorded by Kluster; tracks like "Evas Traum" or "Des Zauberers Traum" could have fallen off Edgar Froese's desk. So, basically, "Eroc" is an adventurous and sonically diverse record worth being rediscovered since it is somewhat forgotten or at least may not come to mind at first when we are talking about kosmische musik nowadays.

Faust: The Faust Tapes (Virgin, 1973)
Famously sold for next to nothing, the record did well in the British charts but nonetheless didn't make any money,

which goes for all the Faust records. The band, hyped by its manager Uwe Nettelbeck as a pop art experiment, was basically a failure. Funny how it goes: now, the records are regarded as holy grails – and for good reason ... The Faust Tapes are the most entertaining record of them all, a cut-up mess, a collage of whatever recordings were left over or at hand back then, all in all sounding like going up and down the frequency band of your fm-radio.

Edgar Froese: Aqua (Virgin, 1974)
The Tangerine Dream mastermind's first solo effort. a dark and dense piece of work far from more accessible subsequent solo-records like "Stuntman" or "Pinnacles", the compositions on "Aqua" function as psycho-active electronic music for introspection, to reconnect with the molecular basics of yourself. Remember, the larger portion of the human body consists of water!

Manuel Göttsching: Inventions for Electric Guitar (Kosmische Musik, 1975)
Everybody's raving about "E2-E4" being the artistic pinnacle of Manuel Göttsching's solo recordings – and, especially, about how this album was musically anticipating trance and techno music. I get it, but if you're averse to electronically derived drum beats

and still cling on to the more free-floating kosmische musik, "Inventions for Electric Guitar" is your go-to record. It's overshadowed by its successor, but that doesn't mean anything, really.

Harald Grosskopf: Synthesist
(Sky Records, 1980)
Harald Grosskopf had already been around when he released his first solo-record: he had played with Wallenstein, in the sessions that led to the Cosmic Jokers / Kosmische Kuriere releases, in later incarnations of Manuel Göttsching's Ash Ra Tempel and on various Klaus Schulze records. Given all that, "Synthesist" sounds like nothing that came before. His approach to drum-accompanied synthesiser music remains visionary and fresh to this day. The record still shimmers just like the artist himself covered in silver paint on the cover of the album.

Guru Guru: UFO (Ohr, 1970)
Another power-trio, another debut, just like the aforementioned first Ash Ra Tempel. The influence of bands like Cream or Jimi Hendrix' Band of Gypsys is evident, but the Blues is missing. Lots of pounding drums, scorching guitars and a pummeling bass. Psychedelic rock music with an emphasis on the mind-blowing freak-out. Bands like the Japanese Acid Mothers Temple and countless others owe it all to Mani Neumeier's trio, which they'll all admit freely, of course.

Peter Michael Hamel: Hamel
(Vertigo, 1972)
As stated above (see "Between"), the composer's work was misunderstood and obscured for a long time. His first solo album is an inspired take on musical ideas of minimalism and the spiritual ideas that accompanied it back then. It mirrors the works of and friendship with Terry Riley and is reminiscent of the experimental recordings Don Cherry released with the Organic Music Society; boundless mesmerising musical creativity in every possible sense of the word.

Harmonia: Musik von Harmonia
(Brain, 1974)
When Michael Rother joined Dieter Moebius and Hans-Joachim Roedelius they recorded two records that display a childlike joy for simple melodies and repetition. The music's not overly complicated, the patterns easy to follow – and that's what makes the music so audacious in its (alleged) naivety. But, of course, it's not that easy to pull off, and the enduring interest in the records are a testament to Harmonia's seducing and soothing musical qualities.

Kalacakra: Crawling to Lhasa
(Private Press, 1972)
Stoner-folk-meditations from Duisburg, located in the populous, then-industrial Ruhr-area of Germany. Music as primitive and escapist and stoned as possible. All you need

is an acoustic guitar, a few percussive instruments, some weed and off you go: "Crawling to Lhasa". Not despite but *because* of its amateurish musicianship, it's an important record and over the decades past it grew a large following which adds to its cult-status.

Jürgen Karg: Elektronische Mythen
(Mood Records, 1978)
The sole electronic music record of jazz musician Jürgen Karg, who recorded "Free Action" (for MPS Records) with the aforementioned Wolfgang Dauner. "Elektronische Mythen" was initially released on Mood Records, a German independent jazz label (very much like the more famous Freie Musik Produktion, FMP). The cover art looks like an outtake from Tarkovsky's "Stalker" and the music sounds indeed like an alternative soundtrack to the movie. It's an oddball release in the label's discography, a stark, bleak and very dissonant recording. Soon after, Karg vanished from the musical landscape, which makes his "Elektronische Mythen" even more mysterious.

Kluster: Klopfzeichen
(Schwann AMS Studios, 1970)
Very much like the Cluster record above, "Klopfzeichen" is a proto-industrial-music record. In comparison to Cluster's debut, it's more vocal and explicit about

its political perspective: "Ich gebe meine Stimme ab, denn ich habe sie nie gebraucht" ("I cast my vote because I never needed it" – "voice" and "vote" are synonymous in German), a disillusioned and devastating comment in the aftermath of the so-called student revolution from 1968. Listening to the record still is a stunning experience.

Kraftwerk: Ralf & Florian (Vertigo, 1973) Still the less clean and not so restrained version of Kraftwerk, the earlier, quirkier and somewhat ramshackle version of the band that nowadays and way too often is only appreciated for anything they released from "Autobahn" on. I recommend embracing and appreciating the early works more – and don't forget the Organisation's "Tone Float" record!

Liliental: Liliental (Brain, 1978) A krautrock supergroup in some respect: featuring the musical talents of famed producer Conny Plank and Cluster's Dieter Moebius, Asmus Tietchens and his frequent collaborator Okko Becker as well as Kraan musicians Helmut Hattler and Johannes Peppert. They recorded one eponymous album and that's it. Doesn't sound like much, but judging by the pictures on the back of the record's cover it was fun to hang out in Plank's rural studio, enjoying the hospitality and recording an enjoyable album of not too challenging electronic music. Fair enough!

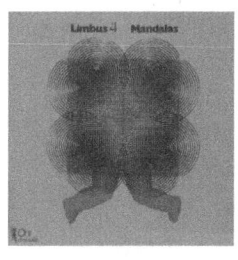

Limbus 4: Mandalas (Ohr, 1970)
Experimental-Psychedelic-Folk from Heidelberg, formerly Limbus 3, then expanding to a four-piece band and releasing one superb album. It's the kind of music that's rare, especially in Germany, in its zoned-out but mild-mannered, rather playful approach. Not as solemn as the – in some respects musically similar, but spiritually and aesthetically more aspiring – Popol Vuh. There's early Amon Düül, Kalacakra, Limbus 4 and not much else (the rather obscure Siloah, maybe, too). Today, bands like Metabolismus carry the torch.

Moebius & Plank: Rastakraut Pasta (Sky Records, 1980)
The first of four collaborative records between Dieter Moebius and Conny Plank. Instrumental post-kraut-industrial-dub-spoken-word-whatever music! Anything goes, nothing to prove, no boundaries. Very much like the Liliental recording sessions, this is the product of a relaxed working atmosphere in Plank's studio, I suppose. Go where the music leads you. Unashamed, unafraid, unapologetic. Holger Czukay joins in on three tracks playing bass.

Musikalische Gruppen-Improvisation: Musikalische Gruppen-Improvisation (Landesarbeitsgemeinschaft Musik, 1971)
Not really a record in the common sense but more a work performance record. The music released on this album is

documenting workshops for music teachers, educators and others interested in not-necessarily-professional musical practice. Recording artists such as Harald Klemm from Annexus Quam and Jürgen Havix (Kollektiv) were involved in improvising and experimenting with curious non- or not-so-skilled folks. The results are far from boring and worth your attention.

Neu!: Neu! (Brain, 1972)
„Two Cool Rock Chicks Listening to Neu" (Ciccone Youth, 1988), and they still listen to "Negativland", the second to last track on the band's debut. Very little from the krautrock aesthetics has proven to be as influential and persistent as the infamous Neu!-beat, the motoric drum pattern, stoic and as non-groovy as a metronome. Quite an achievement!

Popol Vuh: Affenstunde (Liberty, 1970)
Popol Vuh are one of the most unique krautrock bands. More or less the solo endeavour of Florian Fricke, the project's output remains unparalleled. The first two records consist of electronic music mostly made on a Moog synthesiser. "Affenstunde" is a pioneering work. Maybe not on purpose, but nonetheless. Fricke would later move away from electronic music and devote himself

to a unique blend of syncretistic or quasi-religious music, but that's another story.

Pyrolator: Inland
(Warning Records, 1979)
Kurt Dahlke's first solo effort can be seen as a record of experimental electronic music in line with seminal works such as Tangerine Dream's "Electronic Meditations", Kluster's "Klopfzeichen" and Cluster's "71" – rather harsh, atonal and disharmonic sonic improvisations/compositions. It also embodies the post-kraut spirit of post punk and the neue deutsche welle. It's a transitional record, marking an aesthetic watershed.

Riechmann: Wunderbar
(Sky Records, 1978)
Put them side to side and the similarities are striking: Dinger's "Für mich", Grosskopf's "Synthesist" and Riechmann's "Wunderbar" display the same glamorously alien and rather cool look of an androgynous not-so-human-any-more human wrapped up, painted in or surrounded by silvery, shimmering colours. Do these androids dream of electric sheep? Maybe more so of electronic music equipment. Anyway, stunning music. Tragically, this is the only record Riechmann would record before being fatally wounded by a knife attack a few weeks before the album's release.

Hans Joachim Roedelius: Durch die Wüste (Sky Records, 1978)
Roedelius' first solo record was released the same year as Cluster's second collaborative record with Brian Eno (see above). Most of his many solo records have this very recognisable mood: equal parts solemn and strangely upbeat, sentimental, an atmosphere of longing. "Durch die Wüste" already features all the sonic qualities that make Roedelius' sound so distinctive.

Michael Rother: Flammende Herzen (Sky Records, 1977)
Very much like his frequent musical partner Roedelius, Rother's solo recordings inherit a similar taste for the sentimental – in this case one driven towards a dawning horizon by Jaki Liebezeit's drumming. It's undoubtedly uplifting music, music to fall in love with, to enjoy summer and life in general.

Sand: Golem (Delta-Acustic, 1974)
The only record this short-lived group officially released. Much more music would appear decades later on various releases when French label Rotorelief mined the band's archive for unreleased recordings. Anyway, "Golem" is a deeply psychedelic and at times brooding record reminiscent of early- to mid-period Pink Floyd.

There's a general playfulness to the recordings that never explode into massive freak-outs. Instead the band keeps it together, steadily exploring its sonic space.

Günter Schickert: Überfällig
(Sky Records, 1979)
Hypnotic guitar instrumentals that bear similarities to Göttsching's guitar work but in comparison appear less echo-driven or repetitive. The music, especially on the closing track "Wanderer", is dark and meditative, like contemplating a dream shortly after awaking.

Eberhard Schoener: Meditation
(Ariola, 1974)
Eberhard Schoener released a lot of very different music throughout his career as a successful composer, ranging from electronic music to soundtracks for TV series. He owned one of the first (if not the first) Moog synthesisers in Germany, which he had acquired during a trip to the USA from Robert Moog directly (allegedly one that John Lennon had sent back to its inventor). "Meditation" was not recorded on the Moog but realised in the Electronic Studio of the Bavarian Music Studios in Munich. The record's title fits its sonic content, it's emanating gentle sonic waves. At times it sounds like the calm & collected little brother of Tangerine Dream's "Zeit" or a distant academic ancestor to Nurse with Wound's "Soliloquy for Lilith".

Conrad Schnitzler: Con (Egg, 1978)
Having participated in Tangerine Dream's tentative debut and Kluster's equally messy and noisy records, "Con" finds Conrad Schnitzler at his most accessible and straightforward. Only "Metall I" is a reminder of Schnitzler's harsher capabilities, but the majority of the album consists of bubbling and vigorous electronic vignettes, suited for DJ-sets and repeated listening. The closing track "Black Nails" could also function as an alternative soundtrack to a dystopian movie like Carpenter's "Escape from New York". Amazing stuff, altogether.

Klaus Schulze: Timewind (Brain, 1975)
Arguably the poster-boy of kosmische musik and one of its most productive and creative protagonists. His influence can't be overstated and "Timewind", his fifth solo album, is one of many classics in his large catalogue. Switched on Wagner not on Bach, "Bayreuth Return" is a lurking electronic soundscape while "Wahnfried" on the flipside is a much more engaging and aspiring composition neither shying away from nor short of dramatic gestures.

Seesselberg: Synthetik 1.
(Private Press, 1974)
The brothers Wolf-J. and Eckart Seesselberg released one eponymous album that might be considered in the ballpark of Kluster or early Conrad Schnitzler (i. e. "Rot" und "Blau"),

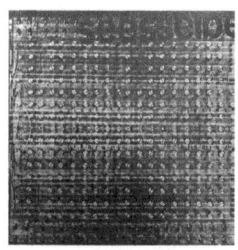
but in comparison, "Synthetik 1" is aesthetically and technically even more prosaic and austere. Music in a decidedly undramatic mode meant as a demonstration of physics and mathematics, which, surprisingly, leads to stunning results.

Karlheinz Stockhausen:
Mikrophonie I – Mikrophonie II
(CBS, 1967)
The Godfather of anything experimental or avant-garde, maybe not just in post-WW II Germany. "Mikrophonie I – Mikrophonie II" was released in 1967 and written three years prior. You don't need to know anything about the composing technics, or the ideas behind it, just listen to the sonic events and the dense atmosphere created and you immediately get what makes this piece of music a pioneering work to this day. Stockhausen eats Wolf Eyes for breakfast.

Tangerine Dream: Alpha Centauri
(Ohr, 1971)
After the sonically fumbling debut, the band around Edgar Froese found its feet with "Alpha Centauri", developing the surreal soundscapes they would be known for in the future. The richly textured music already has this distinct cinematic quality that, by the end of the 1970s, would result in scores to numerous movies throughout the band's long-lasting career.

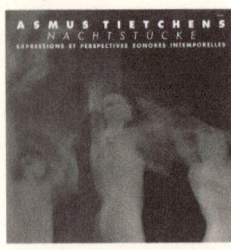

Asmus Tietchens: Nachtstücke (Expressions Et Perspectives Sonores Intemporelles) (Egg, 1980)

Asmus Tietchens may not immediately come to mind when talking about kosmische musik or krautrock, and the musician's catalogue is a varied affair, but "Nachtstücke" in all its DIY-low-key glory is, very much like Riechmann's sole album, a refreshingly modest and deeply charming record. You can't listen to Richard Wahnfried all the time, can you?

Walter Wegmüller: Tarot (Die Kosmischen Kuriere, 1973)

Even though highly recommended, neither Witthüser-Westrupp's incredible stoner-folk nor Sergius Golowin's esoteric storytelling made it onto this list, but Walter Wegmüller's "Tarot" is equally far-out and as unique in its thematic focus as wide-ranging in its musical styles. A double album full of psychedelic promises and prophecies. A holy grail record for a reason.

Xhol Caravan: Electrip (Hansa Record, 1969)

A psychedelic jazz record, active drumming, swirling organ, wailing reeds. As an early entry in the krautrock canon stylistically it's also inheriting bits of that swinging 60s beat-style. A versatile record, krautrock to dance to.

Zweistein: Trip · Flip Out · Meditation
(Philips, 1970)

A fitting title to wrap up this comprehensive list. A release that is over the top from start to finish. Starting with the lavish 3-LP gatefold cover design (reflecting silver foil to resemble a mirror) and continuing with the music which basically aims to musically portray the three stages of a drug trip. Depending on your own perception (drug-fueled or not), the record is totally genius and mind-blowing or a meandering and supposedly boring experience. Who's to decide? Anyway, former schlager singer Suzanne Doucet participated in Zweistein and went on soon after to become a successful new age musician – so, here's another three-step programme for you to follow!

PHOTO CREDITS

Cover, p. 82/83, 89 above: Cluster/Bureau B archive
P. 81, 90 above: Universal Music archive
P. 84/85: Detlef Krenz
P. 86/87: Heinrich Klaffs (https://commons.wikimedia.org/wiki/File:Can_1972_(Heinrich_Klaffs_Collection_102).jpg), https://creativecommons.org/licenses/by-sa/2.0/legalcode
P. 88: Kluster/Bureau B archive
P. 89 bottom: Sky Records archive
P. 90/91 bottom: Jutta Matthes
P. 91 above: Wolfgang Seidel
P. 92/93, 96: Faust/Bureau B archive
P. 94 bottom: Metronome
P. 95: Guru Guru archive

Every effort has been made to trace the copyright holders and obtain permission to reproduce this material. Please do get in touch with any enquiries or any information relating to the rights holder.

Bartel/Gut/Köster (Hg.)
M_Dokumente
Mania D., Malaria!, Matador

Extensive show of works by the three iconographic german underground bands.

The book project "M_Dokumente" focuses on the explicitly female perspective of the all-female bands Mania D., Malaria! and Matador on the West Berlin music and art scene from the late 1970s on.

With oral history documentary by and with Beate Bartel, Gudrun Gut and Bettina Köster as well as contributions by Nick Cave, Diedrich Diederichsen, Christine Hahn, Peter Bömmels, Mark Reeder, Scumeck Sabottka, and Annett Scheffel.

Paperback, 184 pages
German and English
ISBN 978-3-95575-155-5

Hardcover, 192 pages
ISBN 978-3-95575-174-6

szim (Hg.)
Dead Moon
Off the Grid

The documentation tells the entire Dead Moon saga in the words of the band itself. Close friend, author and editor szim spent three summers (2013–2016) in Fred and Toody Coles's attic sifting through photos, flyers and tour diaries, collecting posters and T-shirts and conducting extensive interviews.

This fourth revised and updated edition contains 16 more pages than the third and 36 more pages than the first one. The already extensive photo section now holds even more historical material, posters, flyers as well as an extended and completed discography and gig list. Exclusive to this edition is an interview with Edwin Heath, Dead Moon's longtime tour manager and a detailed view on their musical equipment.

Eric Goulden
A Dysfunctional Success
The Wreckless Eric Manual

In A Dysfunctional Success Eric Goulden writes with an acute eye for detail about growing up in the 60s and 70s in suburban South East England, discovering music and girls; life as an art student in the frozen north-eastern city of Hull; the formation and dissolution of bands with desperate equipment, a homemade ethos and not much idea; his move to London in 1976 and subsequent recording debut on the newly formed Stiff Record label.

This is an honest coming of age story from both sides of instant pop success: bands, squalid flats, menial jobs, making records, his rise to the point of fame and the falling off into poverty and alcoholism in Thatcher's Britain where Goulden ultimately survived the 1980s to achieve his own kind of success.

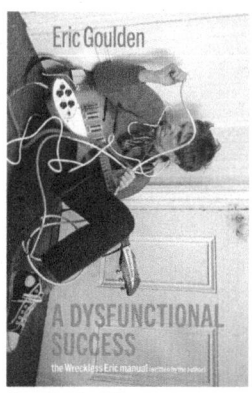

Paperback, 288 pages
ISBN 978-3-95575-223-1

Paperback, 264 pages
ISBN 978-3-95575-178-4

Benjamin Berton
Dreamworld
The fabulous life of Daniel Treacy and his band Television Personalities

London 1977: Daniel Treacy drops out of school, bored to death. With friends, he records a few songs thanks to a few pounds sterling lent to him by his parents and sends the finished single to the legendary radio DJ John Peel, who is immediately thrilled — the Television Personalities are born ...

"Dreamworld" is the very real, very crazy story of a genius in music history. Enriched with plenty of scene and period color from British pop from the 1960s to the present, it tells of all the ups and downs of a legend who was once called the "Godfather of Indie Pop".

With a fully revised color picture section and numerous illustrations.

Thank You For a Lovely Day
11 The Go-Betweens
Songcomics

Pop music and comic culture — somehow they have always been siblings. So what could be more natural than to have the great songs of one of the most legendary bands transformed into comic strips by fantastic illustrators and cartoonists?

So here its is: The Go-Betweens songcomic "Thank You for a Lovely Day". Eleven songs from the entire creative period of the iconic Australian band interpreted by international cartoonists and artists. As diverse, colorful and complex as the band's nine studio albums.

Hardcover, 128 pages
ISBN 978-3-95575-182-1

Hardcover, 192 pages
ISBN 978-3-95575-174-6

Jimi Tenor
Omniverse
Sounds, Sights and Stories

A techno pioneer in the 1990s, Tenor turned primarily to his love of jazz beginning in the 2000s, recording an album with Afrobeat legend Tony Allen, among others, and collaborating with several orchestras. As the first part of the new Sounds, Sights & Stories series, "Omniverse" uses photos and stories to document the various stages of Jimi Tenor's life and career, whose work extends far beyond his music - from photography and filmmaking to instrument making and fashion design, everything is conceivable in the world of what is probably the first Finnish pop star.